PATTERNS OF DESIRE: SEXUAL DIVERSITY IN PSYCHOANALYSIS

PATTERNS OF DESIRE: SEXUAL DIVERSITY IN PSYCHOANALYSIS

WILLIAM G. HERRON
AND
RAFAEL ART. JAVIER

Nova Science Publishers, Inc.
New York

LIBRARY OF CONGRESS CATALOGING-IN-PUBLICATION DATA
Available upon request

ISBN 1-59454-584-7

Published by Nova Science Publishers, Inc. ✢ New York

CONTENTS

PREFACE

This new and important book reformulates the importance of sexuality in psychoanalysis through an integrated theory reflecting contemporary multiculturalism. The disappearance of sex as a drive has been a function of the focus on sex as a relationship. This focus has been a useful antidote to the lack of intersubjectivity that seemed to dominate drive theory, but relational theory has unduly diminished the role of sexual desire. Self-theory has made an attempt to retain a "drive-like" character for sexuality, and in the process made a case for psychic energy, personal agency, and libidinal motivation, but appears to stumble in an excessive emphasis on the power of agency as well as the need to eliminate instinctive causality. This book challenges the prevailing paradigm in psychology in general and psychoanalysis, in particular. That is, the over-reliance on specific theoretical formulations that do not provide adequate opportunities to understand and truly appreciate the dilemma that patients normally bring to a practice.

INTRODUCTION

This book reformulates the importance of sexuality in psychoanalysis through an integrated theory reflecting contemporary multiculturalism. The first chapter highlights the fact that in developing psychoanalysis, Freud was a revolutionary in emphasizing the importance of sexuality. However, this revolution was tempered by restrictions on the expression of sexuality and the need to pathologize sexual options that did not involve heterosexual intercourse as a relationship. Sexual pathways have had their share of stones and boulders since then. A desire for motivational reductionism has limited the understanding of sexuality by primarily depicting sex as either instinctual or relational, in turn slighting patients' experiences. While enjoying initial prominence, the instinctual component has faded relative to a relational emphasis, but neither is adequate as an exclusive explanation. A more comprehensive theory is needed, but, none have gained significant acceptance. Also, unfortunately multidimensionality has been used to lessen the importance of libido by adding motives while subtracting the amount of power attached to each one. This seems like an ironic twist to Freud's economic theory. However, expansionist approaches can be modified to develop a hierarchy of motivation that retains and enhances the importance of sexuality.

The disappearance of sex as a drive has been a function of the focus on sex as a relationship. This focus has been a useful antidote to the lack of intersubjectivity that seemed to dominate drive theory, but relational theory has unduly diminished the role of sexual desire. Self-theory has made an attempt to retain a "drive-like" character for sexuality, and in the process made a case for psychic energy, personal agency, and libidinal motivation, but appears to stumble in an excessive emphasis on the power of agency as well as the need to eliminate instinctive causality. Our view is broader than the original conception of sexuality, but less restrictive than some contemporary theories, as well as more focused in its expansiveness than others. We are suggesting a balanced comprehensive view that restores the recent depletion of the drive component.

In so doing, consideration needs to be given to the relational components of sexuality, and the possibility of an unconscious relational context as motivation. However, the possibility of sensory-driven instinctual experiences that are sexual should also be included. Also, both the presence and continuation of sexual excitement, as well as discharge, are depicted as viable sources of sexual pleasure. One form of sexual activity is not automatically better than another, because sexuality is very much a matter of personal meaning.

Sexuality can definitely be the terrain of whatever comes to mind, despite limits in action. It is a potential playground, serving many aims. At the moment the drive components of sexuality need a revival, with an expansion stressing motivational rebalancing. Sexuality has the potential to bring drives, relations, and other motivations into an integrated system, although the model is likely to have some ragged edges. Nonetheless, a more comprehensive model is possible by combining parts of existing models as well as being innovative.

In Chapter 2 we address the question of gender identity. We begin with Freud's views that anatomy determined gender, but that a differentiated self was not present at birth, so neither was the sense of a gendered self. However, even with the possibility of early self-differentiation, a person's gender is at first learned from others. Subsequent developments have raised the possibility of a core gender identity formed by a number of factors. These appear to be an original polymorphous, pansexuality, which is flexible and selective.

There is a connection between gender identity and the general concept of identification. We view identification resting on the appeal of caregivers as well as their gender. As a result, gender identity is a function of the realities of anatomy and corresponding social and parental designations, as well as attitudes that are incorporated because the self finds them appealing. Anatomical gender is a plan subject to social-cultural-relational influences reflecting personal meanings.

The either-or dualism of the past, as well as gender superiority, appear now as distorted social constructions that resulted in warped concepts of masculinity, femininity, and sexuality. Current evidence suggests an early organizing self along with instinctual sexuality and the potential for the formation of interpersonal interactive systems. The child learns a gender identity and a gender role. Then these are refashioned throughout development. There is a potential fluidity to this process that is in contrast with the inevitability that has often been proposed. The aim is to integrate gender identity and sexuality in an adaptive, satisfactory manner. This often proves difficult because of the intricate meanings attached to masculinity and femininity that become integral to identity. We offer some clinical examples to illustrate the importance of the issue and the need to understand individual sexual development.

Chapter 3 is concerned with gender orientation. The first issue is the meaning attached to the words that describe gender roles and identities. Language usage is problematic in discussing sexuality. For example, we describe issues raised by the use of preference relative to the use of orientation, as well as the reaction to the development of queer theory. Then we discuss how deconstructing gender has altered familiar concepts of male and female, and opened up the concepts of gender bending and gender mixing. We consider the original version of gender identity development, focused on identification and loss, as well as the mixture of biology and psychology. The result was a biological essentialism that reinforced male superiority and made heterosexuality the norm for sexual health. This view has subsequently been subject to alterations by a number of contemporary challenges from feminism, queer theory, and relational and self psychologies.

There has been a recognition of the social construction of gender identities and roles that illustrates the inaccuracy of the previous assumed gender superiority. Homosexuality is no longer automatically viewed as a pathological development. This provides opportunity for the normality of polymorphous sexuality, and markedly expands the consideration of normal pathways to what were previously considered marginalized sexualities.

The changes that have been made have understandably given priority to correcting errors in psychoanalytic theories of sexuality, such as expanding the cultural concerns and decreasing bias toward marginalized sexual and gender preferences. Now we suggest a revised developmental theory that is a psychobiological process including instinctive polymorphous sexuality that is potentially flexible in a multicultural matrix. It is refined through introjection and social interaction to result in the formation of a focused sexuality. Specific interests, preferences, and behaviors are based on personal attractors that are often somewhat mysterious and unpredictable in origin. Clinical examples are presented to illustrate the cultural construction of masculinity and femininity, as well as the problematic meanings often attached to these concepts. Object preferences and inclinations to specific sexual pleasures are considered options rather than choices. While recognizing biological contributions, as instinctive sexuality, favored orientations and behavior represent personal attractions drawn from numerous experiential possibilities. We grant that a diagnostic schema for sexuality could have utility, but, so far, what has been proposed emphasizes pathology for marginalized groups. The results have too often been harmful, so it is more useful to employ specific consideration of sexual behavior in regard to its meaning and effects. Our focus is on the expansion of normative sexual possibilities and appreciation of the pleasure of sexual excitement derived from such diversity.

Chapter 4 begins with consideration of proposed revisions to developmental pathways to healthy sexuality that have been suggested by others. These include sexuality originating as polymorphous and subsequently developing in a focused manner, but these reflect primarily changes in definitions rather than the extensive elaboration now needed. Problematic examples include separating polymorphous from perverse, or suggesting an additional dimension of distinction between phallic and genital. Another example is the promotion of relational sex over personal sexual excitement. As revision, we consider sexuality as best viewed as contextual and contingent, with motivational distinctions leading to different possibilities. Pathways to sexual expression need to focus on understanding all types of sexual expression.

To do this we consider how people establish erotic objects. We start with the preferences learned from caretakers, then consider the apparent meaning of the awareness of anatomical differences, and then the process of internalization that involves introjection, identification, and identity. Sexuality is viewed as instinctually derived with sexual identity being primarily a cultural construction influencing sexual preference. Instead of biological essentialism being a major determinant, sexuality originates as options, many of which are subsequently repressed, so sexual orientation often feels predetermined. However, sexuality is potentially fluid, with the result being primarily a result of personal attractors whose origins are often unconscious, and in turn, may remain unknown. Healthy sexuality requires adaptation, but the degree of restriction also requires revision because it has been excessive. The social pressure for everyone to be heterosexual is a marked example, and changes are happening there.

We discuss the development of the heterosexual norm, based on incorporating the gender preference of the same sex parent. There is an identification with the social construction of being masculine or feminine. However, there are many identifications available for each gender, with personal attractors being the primary determinant for erotic desire. This may conflict with the social learning process that fosters gender-specific socially approved desires and selection of partners.

The mother, by proximity, is the likely first object for erotic feelings and identification for both genders. However, both genders will suffer the loss of parents as erotic objects, and move on to people outside of the family as part of the resolution of the oedipal complex. In addition, the boy's identification with the mother will shift, but not the gender of the erotic object. This follows the heterosexual norm, as does sublimation and repression of polymorphous sexuality.

Of course, all people do not adhere to the heterosexual norm. This indicates they are following different identifications and desires based on personal attractors. These are formed from a mixture of instinct, experience, cultural construction, and the singular appeal of many sources, conscious and unconscious. What prevails are stimuli that are most compelling on an individual basis.

Gay, lesbian, and bisexual patterns can have similar healthy developmental pathways using the same internalization processes as heterosexuality. All these types of sexuality can be defensive as well, as we have illustrated in clinical examples. Sexual activities that are unusual are a function of personal attractors akin to those reflecting different sexual identities. In a further consideration of the defensive aspects of sexuality, a distinction is drawn between sexual problems and sexual offenses. There is often some overlap in behavior creating difficulty in determining what is sexual pathology.

Queer theory is elaborated as a relatively fresh approach to the understanding of sexual diversity. This is followed by a summary of the development of psychoanalytic theories of erotic preferences that begins with the traditional family model and repression of diversity in service of the heterosexual norm. Then challenges to this norm are noted. Greater attention needs too be devoted to the theoretical formulations of healthy, adaptive, sexual diversity. This requires analytic explorations of the origins of personal attractors based on powerful individualized conscious and unconscious influences.

In the final chapter we draw together our revisionist suggestions and offer an integrated model for understanding sexuality. We describe essential building blocks for a metapsychology. The first is the multiplicity of motivation rather than reductionism. Sexuality is a significant motive among an undesignated number of possibilities. Sexuality varies in quantity and quality for each person, and is instinctually and experientially originated.

Sexuality has an aim of both excitement and discharge, and is a psychobiological experience with the potential of over determination.

Then, we consider sexuality originating as a diverse desire in regard to both object preference and activity. Sexual orientation is primarily influenced by the process of internalization with ego and superego factors affecting the expression of desire, itself shaped by personal attractors. Conflict appears when desire is restrained by reality or social constructions.

Normal patterns of development exist for diverse sexual orientations. Differences appear in personal attractors and styles of identification. Sexual behavior needs to be understood as individualized with the analytic process an ideal way for such exploration. The clinical goal is enabling each person to achieve the most acceptable sexual expression. The analyst and patient need to develop an awareness of sexual acceptability in order to comprehend and enhance the patient's sexuality within that frame. This involves an exploration of sexual motives, primarily sensory appeal and symbolic personal meaning. Sexuality is over-determined, with variable specifics in expressing desire.

Rather than classifying sexuality in any designated schema, it is useful to explore personal history to understand favored approaches and their motivations. This results in understanding what is problematic as well as what is adaptive, and makes change possible. Sexuality includes conflict and resolution in the formation of a preferred orientation and behaviors. These tend to become customary, but are potentially flexible, reflecting the original diversity of sexuality.

In addition to the sexual conflicts of patients, there is the problem of the countertransference of the analyst arising from personal sexual needs that interfere with the analytic work. We highlight four examples, followed by taking notice of a more general reaction of anxiety about sexuality that has unfortunately and unnecessarily limited the expression of desire. We end by suggesting that psychoanalysis be a primary force in promoting understanding and appreciation of sexual diversity.

In writing this book we had a large amount of clinical material available to us through our own work with patients, supervisory work, and discussions with colleagues. We distilled this so that we were able to create pertinent clinical illustrations for our ideas. In all cases, we have made a major effort to disguise identities and events so that confidentiality is maintained.

We speak with one voice in this book. I, William G. Herron, particularly enjoyed the reflective exchanges with my co-author as we fashioned a distinctive portrait of sexuality. His involvement in a project so intriguing to me was exceptionally valuable. Major credit also goes to Mary Jane Herron, my wife, who is truly wise about sexual matters. She has always shared that wisdom with me, and fortunately, I have paid attention. In turn, I dedicate this book to the outcome of an exceptional sexual understanding, our daughters, Abigail and Allison, on the genesis of their careers, the former in psychiatry, the latter in law.

It was an enjoyable experience for me, Rafael Art. Javier, because the book challenges the prevailing paradigm in psychology in general and psychoanalysis, in particular. That is, the over-reliance on specific theoretical formulations that do not provide adequate opportunities to understand and truly appreciate the dilemma that our patients normally bring to our practice. What we are calling for is the return to a more scholarly stance, where judgment is truly suspended and the patient is then allowed to reveal the true nature of his/her sexuality in all its components. This is particularly important in view of the culturally diverse patient population whose view of sexuality and sexual behavior may be different than ours and where the tendency to pathologizing their experience is ever so great. I would like to thank my co-author for his scholarship and determination in making this book possible. My students Danielle Rannazzisi, Jennifer Salhany and Lorie J. Blas deserve special thanks for their assistance in putting the manuscript together. We hope that the readers enjoy the book as an invitation to a constructive dialogue where the patient becomes again the center of the inquiry and where the concepts of health and pathology are determined from the multiplicity of information derived from the patient's unique history.

Chapter 1

CREATION OF DESIRE

SEXUAL REVOLUTION

The psychoanalytic view of sexuality was probably the "big bang" of its times, but for many years it had a following only about the size of the group that today know the story of *Hedwig and the Angry Inch.* We consider the founder, Sigmund Freud, to be a revolutionary on the scale of Karl Marx, but with more modest aims, and a far more pleasant style of writing. Probably to Freud's amazement, would he today glimpse a DVD summary of how his hypotheses turned out, he would see they had an extraordinarily powerful and culturally widespread impact.

Despite biographies, we remain attached to the question of Freud's unrevealed desires, just as we wonder about the intrinsic and extrinsic qualities of Lacan's phallus that nobody seems to own but anybody can imagine. We do know that Freud's goals were similar to that of many scientists, namely to discover the causes and cure for certain diseases. His targets were the mysterious mental disorders, and in the beginning, only a handful of them. He started with conversion hysteria, and focused on neuroses. This is now a term, which despite its historical significance, fascinatingly has essentially disappeared from the official psychiatric nomenclature. This illustrates the need to be careful about the use of words, but in this case, Freud really has had the last word because the disorders live on.

In attempting to solve the then unfathomable problems of the neuroses, he created a very different, unexpected way of investigation and treatment. In so doing, he essentially brought psychoanalysis on line. Over time, psychoanalysis has evolved into a culture of its own which shapes, and is shaped, by the cultures in which it operates as well as the ethnicities it serves. Contained within the psychoanalytic culture is a very elaborate theory of sexuality, which is at the center of this book.

One of the most significant contributions of this theory has been illustrating to the world that sexuality is far more important as a motive and a cause for behavior than most people had acknowledged or were willing to admit. An essentialist approach to Freud's theories is that everything is ultimately about sex, even when that does not appear to be the case. This was a radical concept when proposed approximately a century ago in *Three Essays on the Theory of Sexuality* (Freud, 1905). It still is, and sex remains a relatively taboo topic, despite liberalization. Freud's proposals were met with considerable disbelief, as well as bitter opposition and ridicule. Such attacks may have contributed to his limitations in listening to sympathetic dissenters. At the same time he was able to develop a pre-Kohutian way of appropriating good ideas of others, including the unsympathetic. The result was the development of a comprehensive theory that went beyond sexual relationships. It involved a detailed metapsychology, and he continually revised his theoretical propositions in a variety of ways. However, and this is a key feature for our concerns, he remained attached to the preeminence of libido. Although psychoanalysis wasn't evolving in the direction of being all about sex, it was very much about sex.

Freud was at the entry point of a wave of social changes, particularly the alteration of a family system that relied on gender stereotypes and sexual conformity. These were not issues he had set out to change, yet his theorizing provided greater possibilities for changes that were already progressing. As Kaplan (1997) notes, the bourgeois family was fading in the face of increasing gender ambiguity and a social order that was far more welcoming to erotic expression. Freud offered a theoretical underpinning for making alterations by emphasizing sexuality, at the same time that he did have rules that could pathologize certain sexualities as well as reinforce rigid gender roles.

Freud repositioned sex, and at the same time began something that has long since outrun his intentions. His desires that the true importance of sexuality be recognized have become more realized in all societies and among all ethnic groups, although sexual repression is more prominent in some cultures than in others (Francoeur & Noonan, 2004). The premise of Freud's Western European sexuality, namely the singular importance of sex in human behavior, is a universal facet of the human condition. Also, while psychoanalysis provided a more open forum for discussing and understanding sexuality, a strong component of the theory has been discovering the appropriate expression of sexuality. In the main, that has emphasized heterosexual intercourse, in terms of the importance of anatomical differences as complementary to the execution of the act, and relatively circumscribed gender roles. Anything else usually has been depicted as abnormal or transitory and pathologized in some fashion. For too long such an emphasis has signified that the theory needs modification.

At the same time there has been considerable expansion of sexual knowledge, but coming primarily from sources outside the psychoanalytic community (Money, 1990). Although psychoanalysis has remained the most comprehensive theory of sexual development, it has unfortunately failed to keep pace with the current knowledge base of sexual experience. A concerted effort has not occurred to link new information regarding sexuality with an encompassing theory of sexual development. Furthermore, despite the greater availability of sexual knowledge in all cultures and societies, the more prominent psychoanalytic theories of sexuality have promoted what we call "social sex" in which instinct and drive are subsumed under attachment, connection, and relationships.

Greenberg (1991) has suggested that the alternatives to Freud's dualism are theories without drives, a single drive theory, and theories of motivation that contain multiple drives. In a trenchant criticism, he notes that theories striving to eliminate the concept of drive, conceptually appear to contain a drive construct, though it is deliberately not called "drive." We would add that the most prominent single-drive theories are prone to see relating as the "driving" motivational force, which leaves sex on the sidelines. Greenberg prefers a dualism, though not Freud's, and he buries libido somewhere within a safety-effectance model. He dismisses multiple drive models as conceptually flawed. In contrast, we are impressed with the idea of motivational expansion contained in the multiplicity of drives, provided that sexuality is not overshadowed. What concerns us in drive expansion is that there is a move away from the importance of sexuality to make room for some other possibly neglected, yet important, motivation. Actually, this diminution of sex has gotten some notice (Dimen, 2003; Green, 1996), but it tends to prevail. We want to change this by restoring the vitality of sex and expanding the understanding of its diversity.

Social sex reflects an understandable deemphasis of a principle of libidinal dominance that left unanswered questions about key roles played by a variety of motivational possibilities neglected by drive reductionism. At the same time, such a benign sexual theory unduly limits sensuality in the midst of an intensely sexual world. Any insistence on understanding sexuality as having to be within the context of a relational world neglects a significant portion of sexual experience. As Winnicott (1965) suggested, there is not merely a self, but selves, namely a personal self and an interactive self. These resonate with the idea of a private sexuality and relational sex, coexisting and variable human attributes.

Fonagy and Target, summarizing interpersonal-relational approaches, state, "Sexuality is not seen as a push from within, even if it is experienced this way;..." (2000, p.214).

We call attention to the word, "experienced," because it is the experience that requires explanation. To downplay the patient's experience seems ironically to represent the one-person psychology that so disturbs the relational approach, yet it seems to appear when sex is the issue. Of course, both by dialogue and authoritative one-person interpretation , distortions of experience can be revealed and clarified in analysis, but that differs from denying the feeling quality of the experience. To clarify the difference, let us first hypothesize that sexuality is not primarily a push from within, but a person feels as if it is. To us this seems sufficient clinical data to refute any assumption that that the internal push cannot exist. It then seems that an exclusive interpersonal explanation is an inadequate depiction of an internal sexual urge that may be reported, and felt as unrelated to objects or devoid of a fantasized object attachment. Let us put it this way. It happens.

As a result, one-horse theories about sexuality do not adhere sufficiently to patient experience. This is true for theories that rely on object-ties to motivate sexual desires and it is true for theories insisting on placing objects in the category of mere instruments for discharging sexual impulses. A more comprehensive theoretical and clinical approach is needed.

To further illustrate the complexity of sexual desire, let us consider an example in which objects are involved, but relationships appear secondary to the display of a sexual urge. A man recalls that since childhood he has exposed himself to women and masturbated as he did this. According to his account, most of the women leave the area once they become aware of his exposure. Others have attempted to ignore him, while a few have responded by exposing themselves. Whatever the women did, he always responded the same way, which was to masturbate until ejaculation. Recently, as an adult, he was caught and arrested, and then psychologically evaluated. The evaluator attributed his actions to the dynamics within the family, namely his method of shocking and embarrassing his parents and siblings, and in turn, a way to gain a perverse type of self-esteem.

The explanation is plausible, but is it appropriate to consider the orgasms relational, given that people were involved in some fashion? More pointedly, is this sex in a relational context because it involved, at least at the onset, the presence of another person? His fantasies are important in attempting to answer the questions. His primary fantasy was of an explosive orgasm that covered the page of a book, so he always carried out his actions where there were books as well as women. In fact, he was arrested in a library. The significance of the books wasn't clarified, but the primacy of this fantasy seems to move the motive away from a clearly relational setting. Also, his orgasms took place regardless of the continued presence of the women, so it would appear as if an internal push prevailed. Here the instinctive and relational developmental lines appear to be interactive rather than exclusionary. Both settings, women and books, as well as the physical satisfaction of the orgasm, bear scrutiny.

Taking another step, let us inquire about the relational possibilities in nocturnal emissions. These may or may not be accompanied by dreams in connection with the sexual discharge. They are a bodily process, not obviously relational, but open to the possibility of unconscious fantasies of others as part of the process. In fact, as we will show later in the book, the unconscious is a handy tool when one wishes to assign a cause or motivation that isn't obvious from stated evidence. It is not, however, the most tangible proof of a position, given by definition it has an elusive relationship with awareness. If there are no such fantasies, however, which also has to be considered possible, these emissions could be biological functions akin to urination.

Sex can be experienced as working by itself, working on the subject of the person, carrying out the commands of a biological self. Sex can also be experienced as working with others, real or imagined. There is also the self as agent within an intrasubjective experience of a bodily self with a type of psychic dialogue among parts of the self as sexual experiences. Other possibilities could be conceptualized as well, all of them supporting our assertion of the encompassing nature of sexuality.

Patients' experiences are what command attention and open possibilities. For example, the concept of an internal push is described as body tyranny by Phillips (1998). It is not sufficient to just stretch existing theory to somehow account for what neither patients or analysts seem able to understand. Much is unknown and varying portions of it may stay that way during the course of an analysis. That is frustrating, but likely, and no excuse for limiting the search for theoretical and clinical understanding. Reductionism can result in such limitations, either by exclusion, or by an apparent expansion of motivations which essentially diminishes the role of a motive through making it a component of a broader, and supposedly more important motive. Single and dual drive theories represent the first type of reductionism, whereas certain multidimensional theories illustrate the second. However, the odds favor the accuracy of multidimensional approaches, provided they include different arrangements in each person of motivational primacy, as well as being open to the number and quality of motivations. Admittedly a messy solution, but it is the most accurate fit for sexual experience. In fact, an example of this approach is already appearing in some descriptions of the overall clinical experience. Credence is being given to both the presence of the "third" in the consulting room as well as the quality of the experience. This is an expansion of the factors involved in the analytic dialogue. In turn, then, it is appropriate to recognize and understand the "third" (or fourth, or fifth) in regard to sex.

THE DISAPPEARANCE OF DRIVE

We have taken notice of drive substitution, which appears to drain the eros out of libido by renaming and reframing the original drives. As a result, the sexual person indeed rides a pale horse. Mitchell (1988) has provided a comprehensive picture of the difficulties with drive theory as formulated by Freud, and the problems associated with the modifications proposed by those who wanted to deemphasize or discard drive theory, yet remain within a Freudian tradition regarding the importance of sexuality. He also takes note of the theorists who made a more distinctive break from drive theory. When that happens, the importance of sexuality is inevitably diminished.

However, Mitchell comments, "While it is true that infantile sexuality, like sexuality in general, has been underplayed by most relational-model theorists, this is more a historical artifact than a necessity dictated by the premises of the model" (1998, p. 92).

It may be true that the model doesn't have to de-emphasize sexuality just because it is suggested as an alternative to drive theory, but it is difficult to see how it would not detract from the original focus of sexuality. Relational theory is a substantive addition to the understanding of sexual interaction, but the addition loses value if it is used as a substitute. Insistence on being an alternative rather than an expansion takes away from the integration that is possible through the focus on the role of the other. These theories are far better viewed as complementary possibilities, despite problems that have been encountered in attempts at rapprochement.

Another possibility is posed by Rizzuto, Meissner, and Buie (2004). Their concern is primarily with understanding aggression, but it is applicable to sexuality. The idea of sexuality as an internal force seems to create notable discomfort among people who aren't drive theorists. That discomfort appears in emphasizing self-capacities stimulated by specific conditions that are not specified when it comes to sex. Instead, sexuality is considered a function of the self as agent, which implies a level of control beyond what seems consistent with what at times appears to be an uncontrollable force.

Actually, when it comes to the idea of a "force," they seem more comfortable with aggression. They do an impressive job in retaining psychic energy as an action potential They even consider libidinal energy as a motivation, but dispute its conceptualization as a causal force. That role is retained for the self, which, akin to the unconscious covers a lot of ground that is otherwise difficult to explain. If the self as an agent is what they have in mind, that often fits for sexual expression, but it is not congruent with involuntary, bodily-based sexual experience, namely sex as motive and cause.

If the self were to be used to depict the entire person, which it often is, the description is so broad that it requires the designation of components for an explanatory solution, such as agent, subject, or object. Actually the promotion of the self-as-agent has an appeal in that it mitigates the sweeping nature of co-construction. This idea has become ascendant in depicting clinical exchanges. The result is an unwieldy blurring of the responsibilities of analyst and patient. However, our enthusiasm has to be restricted because self-agency is unreceptive to people at times feeling that they are ruled by their instincts, which indeed might just be the case. It is insufficient to conclude that experience is a form of self organization generated by self-interpreted stimulation. More likely is the possibility that part of all personal organization contains biologically-based instinctual components that can feel overwhelming. In fact, they can act that way and require considerable effort, not always successful, for control. Thus, as Freud sagely noted, there is this eternal struggle.

Attunement with the self-descriptive language and body actions that people use to describe themselves, strongly suggest that a certain portion of sexual experience is most accurately described as a drive. This means that a sexual urge is felt as coming from within, has an involuntary character seeking satisfaction, and is narcissistically motivated. In addition to being considered spatially, as a quantitative experience, this component of sexuality can be considered temporally, namely as a drive some of the time. Such an arrangement coexists as a potential with sexual stimulation derived from relationships and the presence and fantasy of others. Overall then, sexuality is experienced as having both drive and relational components varying in intensity and sensory thresholds. To think otherwise does not provide sufficient explanation for the nature of the experience observed in human interactions, including in patients.

How does this conception fit with the original psychoanalytic views of sexuality? Drive was presented then as an instinctual motive and cause with inherent energy exerting pressure to be discharged. The discharge was designed to release tension to derive satisfaction. Libido was its own agent with its own energy, a force that dominated behavior and demanded satisfaction. Not meeting the demand, or directing it inappropriately, posed the risk of neurotic symptoms. This now appears to have been a narrow conception that slighted the role of both relations and the agency of the self because of a postulated connection to evolutionary theory and because of selective cultural norms.

How does our view fit with major theoretical revisions? Over time there have been enough serious objections to instinctual sex to warrant reformulation, but not to warrant dispensing with drive or instinct as a basic part of sexuality. We do not have a predelection for drive theory that we know of, but remain aware that all analysts listen in different ways to patient experience. What we hear and observe is that intermittently, but nonetheless consistently, patients experience sexuality as an internal striving and as devoid of object-ties. In essence, "raw sex" and "processed sex" coexist.

Meissner (1993) attempts to account for such patient data by differentiating drive from a psychic capacity rooted in biology and activated by stimulating motivations. This appears to be a redefinition of drive as motivation still containing the impulsive character embodied in the original conception of drive. In this view, patients' experiences may be"drive-like," but their experiences are not caused by drive as originally defined. Instead, motivation requires the self as a causal agent. This explanation seems to be a strained effort to get rid of drive and keep it at the same time. In fact, (Meissner, 1999) then offers a broad view of the self including involuntary and unconscious behavior. However, there remains an insistence on sexual needs not being caused by drives (Rizzuto, et al., 2004).

The theory of a heterogeneous self that is capable of complex and contradictory levels of functioning fits well with what we are postulating. It is a way of including what appears to be instinctual about sexuality, but the elimination of instinctual drives as causal agents doesn't fit well with our impressions. Why does a drive component have to be defused or supposedly extinguished when it still seems to be quite alive under the umbrella of the self system? We actually agree with the modification of drive power, and with the unlocking of an inevitable agency that suggest a sexual drive devoid of a sexual self. However, instinctual sex seems to be viewed as a threat to the desired autonomy of the self-system. Meissner hears rain when we do not, so out comes the umbrella while the sun is still shining.

We consider self-agency as a reflective activity, akin to what has been described as mentalization (Fonagy, Gergely, Jurist, & Target, 2002). This reflective function is a variable developmental understanding of personal experience, particularly the subjective meaning of affects. As such it can be in conflict with instincts, which requires control to ultimately mesh with the self system. Thus sexual feelings can seem mindless at times in terms of their origins and disruptive until they are processed and integrated within a person. This threat to autonomy seems congruent with distinguishing between subjectivity and the self-a-agent. It also fits with a concern about overdoing co-construction. It calls for a clearer view of the functions of the self-system, but in that context, extracting the drive component from sexuality and replacing it with sexual desire as a function of the self as the agent is more of a wish to be rid of a term than it is a satisfactory explanation of how sexuality operates. The self-system has limited autonomy, restricted by inevitable conflicts in which instinct plays a role. To whatever degree co-constructions do occur, they are also restrictions on individual agency. The same view can be applied to instincts. They exist, and they need control.

Meissner (2000) plays with the concept of the self in a way that is reminiscent of Freud's original use of the ego as interchangeable with the self. Freud found it too restrictive a view, so without much explanation, the self became the whole person and the ego took on a powerful life of its own. Meissner also needs to make some modifications with the self, namely to have a self-system which substitutes self-agency for drive direction. This fits with the self as superagent, but really seems to just recast drive causality rather than expunge it. For example, libido is shifted from a drive that seeks discharge to a mental capacity that is self-activated under "specifically libidinal stimulus conditions" (Rizzuto, et al., 2004, p.78). Also, the self has impulsive functions, so despite the nimble use of words worthy of Lacan, we are back to the idea that sexuality has an instinctual component, can operate as a drive, and in so doing does not require object-related desires. Inherent drive functions exist as potentials in all peoples at all times. Sexuality is an example of a libidinal drive. Replacing it with other terms isn't a satisfactory way to explain the totality of sexual experience. Of course, the biological basis of sexuality is recognized in contemporary theorizing, but diminished, even more in favor of relational emphasis than self-agency. This can be understood as redressing the once-prevalent emphasis of biological influences, but distorts sexual experience in favor of social construction. It may well be that in attempting to correct the more obvious errors regarding sexuality, the feelings of the wronged prevail. As a result the actual sexual experience no longer remains open to full examination. Money (1999) has made the point that sexual development originates in ontogenetics and phylogenetics, both of which depend on biological and social stimulation. Discourse needs to be focused on understanding the relative influence of these contributors to the sexual experience.

SEX WITHOUT OBJECTS

As relational theorists turned drive theory pretty much upside down by considering people to be primarily innately social rather than sexual, let's consider the possibility that it was never such a dichotomy. People can also be innately sexual and still have a distinction between social and sexual relations. These innate qualities are more accurately viewed as potentials because people vary in their degree of socialization and sexuality, as well as using these to serve other needs, as power (Herron, 1999). Sexuality and socialization are not subsidiaries, a point that bears emphasis because at times socialization seems to be about to swallow sex. Instinct has gotten to be a target of eradication in some relational circles, but, as noted, sexual desires and interests exist that are not related to others.

For example, a patient states, "I am just feeling very sexual today."

The analyst asks the patient to tell him more about this feeling. The patient describes how strong the feeling is, "practically overwhelming."

The analyst asks the patient what he is thinking about as he has this feeling.

The response is, "How good it feels."

The emphasis thus far is on the "feeling", but sexual feelings are somewhat different than emotions as customarily described, joy or sadness for example, where the affective component is clear. Feeling sexual is more likely to be experienced as a tension or excitement that 'is bodily-based and originates with limited cognitive development.

The analyst asks if this feeling makes the patient want to do something sexual. The patient replies that it could, and then constructs a sexual fantasy about having intercourse with a woman he saw on the street as he was coming to the analyst's office. Now cognition accompanies sensation and another person is involved. Sexuality has become socialized in fantasy. However, originally the patient's sexual experience was a solitary, somatic creation, objectless by not including the image or presence of another.

Or so it seems.

The patient could have been operating throughout in an unconscious relational context that generated the sexual feeling. Mitchell (1988) asserts that the significance of sexuality lies in the relational meaning attached to the physiological sensations. The body provides a metaphor for relationships. Sexuality reflects the variety of object connections, and in this case, with a little questioning from the analyst. Indeed there is the fantasy of connection to another person, though it might be a stretch to consider the patient thinking about a relationship. The potentiality for sexuality existing as a vehicle to relate can be established, as well as the possibility that the need to relate is what motivates the presence of sexual feelings. The neatly available unconscious is required to do this however, and the possibility remains that the patient's desire originated as he expressed, without objects, and even without an unconscious relational context.

Yes, but could he have been defending again such a context? Again, when it comes to the unconscious, much is possible, even probable, but to reach such a conclusion requires a belief in a universal social need that absorbs all sexuality. This is as much of an assumption as a universal sexuality that includes all sociability. These are ideas that people favor as motivational explanations, but there is not convincing clinical evidence to support them, unless one has them in advance and makes the data fit, which, as we know is psychic cheating.

So, with all that in mind, let us explore the other side. The man had a sensory-driven instinctual experience. This does not mean there is an automatic connection between the presence of sexual tension and a need to release. There is a pleasure in this excitement and in maintaining it. There is pleasure in discharge, but also the loss of the excitement. Thus sometimes the goal may be the maintenance of the excitement, rather than the discharge. The appeal of this tension was originally noted by Edith Jacobson (1964), and recently affirmed by Dimen (2003).

There is also a gender difference in the drive-discharge model. Money (1999) supports the idea that orgasm is not required for sexual enjoyment, and that such a situation is more prevalent in women than men. Women's sexuality does not appear so tied to tension discharge. Women do not have an inevitable refractory phase where sexual excitement is decreased by orgasms, as men do, and are far more capable than men of having multiple and frequent orgasms. Thus men appear to be able to have an orgasm more often and with less effort than women, but when women have orgasms readily, they can have multiple orgasms and maintain a high level of sexual excitement regardless of the frequency of their orgasms. Without alleging reasons for these differences, it would seem that men might ration their orgasms to maximize their pleasure, while women would have as many orgasms as they could whenever they have the opportunity. However, the usual situation is different. For a variety of reasons many women turn out to be anorgasmic. Having an orgasm is work, which limits the pleasure and may cause them to pass up the possibility. In contrast, men are often focused on having an orgasm, and quickly. Social expectations play a major role here. Men are taught to view orgasm as an achievement, despite its reduction of sexual excitement. Women are taught to show limited interest in sexual pleasure. There is an unfortunate enactment of stereotyped versions of masculinity and femininity. In some cases there are emotional or physiological problems, issues discussed later in the book.

For both genders a sexual cycle begins with an excitement phase, but does not have to involve tension release to provide pleasure. It also does not have to be relationally motivated or involve others. The fact that sexual experience is customarily viewed as sexual intercourse resulting in orgasms that involve two people, and that this is often what does happen, does not eliminate other possibilities. An accurate model accounts for diversity without pathologizing possibilities other than male-female sexual intercourse.

In addition to the limitations of drive and relational models as exclusive explanations of sexuality, self-agency is restricted in determining the sexual aims, which can be sublimated, focused on delay or discharge, or be subject to bodily and environmental circumstances that affect outcome. Sometimes sexuality is at the service of a person's wishes, but at other times the body or the mind refuse to cooperate. When the latter occurs, the self is a passive agent, which is not the meaning usually attributed to self-agency. For example, a man intends to masturbate as a means of stimulation prior to having intercourse, but does not plan to have a discharge while stimulating himself. He miscalculates his somatic reaction and ejaculates unintentionally. Or, a woman engages in intercourse with the intention of having an orgasm, but is unable to do so.

The degree of sexual variability illustrates the possibilities for distortion in granting primacy or exclusivity to instincts, relational matrices, self agency, or any other major motivation in attempting to understand sexuality. Add to the interpersonal variations the diversity of sexual patterning on an interpersonal level, and it is clear that more extensive exploration and explanation are needed. Despite the potential complexity, it is clear that the centrality of sexuality is best served by expansive explorations that consider all the experiential patterns that can be observed. This means reevaluation of the appropriate meaning and role of concepts such as desire, instinct, connection, attachment, subjectivity, and mutuality.

We have already noted the need to free drive from an inevitable connection to discharge. In addition, sexual pleasure can be achieved without an apparent connection to others. Also, when there are connections the sexual pleasure achieved is not automatically better because it adds the potential for additional motives and their satisfaction, such as intimacy and intersubjective mutuality. Nor is it worse because of the possible intrusion into the narcissism of the self. It can be different than an act of sexual self-gratification because another person is present, but the personal experience is not necessarily altered by the physical presence of the other. The experienced existence of an object, and a relationship, in a sexual encounter, depends on the creation of mental representations of the object and the relationship.

One possibility, no representation, no object, no relationship.

More likely, there are representations. Images may emphasize the object as the person satisfying the subject's needs, or there may be a focus on the needs of the other, or there may be a mixture of subjective and intersubjective perspectives. Sexual intercourse usually involves one of these three types of activity, with the possibility of alternating perspectives.

There is still another possibility, a variation on the disappearance of the object due to the limitations involved in creating representations of another. The object is not a part of complementarity or symmetry, but a part of the subject. The result is the creation of pseudo-objects, really many subjects where the subject appears as the object as well as the subject.

For example, a woman explains her feelings while she was having sexual intercourse with a man.

"I did not think of him at all. There must be something wrong with that. I mean I was not hallucinating. I know someone was there I suppose, you know, when we began."

"He left?"

"Yes, well left my mind because I am sure if I checked I would have found him."

"All right. He was there at the same time that he wasn't." "I suppose. I really felt like he wasn't there."

"Who was there?"

"I was, with a penis inside of me, a two-headed one actually. Which was mine, attached to me, moving in and out under my control. Weird, but that was it. I was having intercourse with my own penis, with one head that I could imagine, visualize, inside of me, and the other head sticking out. I could see it, just as though it was my penis."

"What do you think this means?"

"What do I think it means? What do you think it means?"

"I don't know."

'You don't? But you have an idea. Penis envy, right?"

"I don't know."

'You don't know a lot."

'Two-headed penis. What can I say about it? It was yours. You were having intercourse with yourself."

"Yes, and God, it was phenomenal."

There is much that can be made of the women's description of her experience, as well as her interaction with the analyst, but they will have to be bypassed in favor of our main aim in describing the material. As the sexual interaction proceeded with another person, the woman experienced herself as subject and object. There was another person there, yet there was not, Instead, there was a subject with both agency and receptivity. The usual state of subjectivity in which there is space between the self and the other (Benjamin, 1998) seems to have been dislodged temporarily.

Sexuality is an opportunity for the unthinkable to be thought, and expressed within some limits, but there's quite a bit of latitude. Play can reign, a pleasant thought. Sex with the other can become sex with the self as whatever is needed from the other is appropriated by the self without having to feel any theft was involved. The sexual self can have as many selves as desired, and objects can be dissolved despite their presence, or for that matter, created in their absence. Sexual experience is so close to dreaming, with all the special, illogical thinking and feeling states of the dream where the unconscious seems to keep tipping into conscious and secondary thought, but will never really surrender the secrets of primary process. One of these is intimacy, which is what makes sex as relating so intriguing.

By emphasizing the need to refocus on the role of instinct and drive in sexual experience, we are trying to limit the primacy of any model. At the moment relational models have gained special prominence, so they will appear as a special concern. Their focus results in our taking issue with seeing sexuality within an interactive context, if that is the only way it is to be viewed and entirely cut loose from its connection to drives. Instead , we believe sexuality requires a multiple model embracing contradiction, dissociation, splitting, and all kinds of apparently unreasonable maneuvers. Its metaphorical possibilities are numerous, and its subject-object connection frequent as well as open to considerable nuance and interpretation. Certainly sexual expression serves aims other than the discharge of libidinal energy. The expression of aggression is an obvious example. Activity and passivity, the classical designations of masculinity and femininity, are basic to sexual experience without being gender-specific. Sexual experience can be so many things, motive, cause, aim, pleasure, disruption, or part of another motive, such as aggression. If the analyst listens with openness to the patient's experience, the possibilities may well seem endless, and interminably amazing.

One understandable reaction to the numerous possibilities is a strong interest in reductionism. The lack of a consensual framework creates a desire to make order out of an apparently chaotic mess. Although it is tempting to try to shrink-wrap sexuality, we have to keep cautioning against that and reinforcing the idea of living with the messiness. This view is supported by Dimen(2003) as she makes a convincing case for contingency rather than determinism, multiplicity instead of reductionism, and the messiness of sexuality, which is more than a metaphor.

At the same time, we can try to sift through the messiness without losing its flavor and see if we cannot produce a relative working model for the many patterns of sexuality. The sexual experience has a minimal requirement of biological responsivity that is stimulated by something. This can be internal or external to the person. It does not have to be a person, or a fantasy involving people, or direct physical stimulation. At different times in one's life the sexual response overloads or is underpowered. When overloaded the excitement level is high and there is an urge to discharge that, at times, operates without conscious volition. When underpowered, despite a wish for sexual arousal or discharge, the body will not comply. There is an apparent lack of sexual energy. The word, "energy," is used in accord with Meissner's view that psychic energy is a useful concept, despite its resistance to specific definition. We agree with him that there is a need for an economic principle in psychoanalysis (Rizzuto, et al., 2004) to account for the person's capacity to respond to stimulation in various ways. The limitations of Freud's original energy model do not rule out a concept of psychic energy or make it a metaphor only. The person embodied is using neurophysiological energy to function, and that energy has quantitative and qualitative aspects that add up to a concept of psychic energy whose precise definition remains elusive, but the name still seems to fit.

In support of psychic energy there is the relationship of brain mechanisms to expression in both affect and motivation (Danasio, 1999; LeDoux, 1996). Psychic life is a psychological concept with organic foundations, but it is not considered reducible to brain activities. The knowledge of specific brain activities is quite limited, and brain development has a dependency on relational experiences as part of the connection between emotional development and the growth of brain mechanisms. There is a psychic organization of biopsychological motivations. In that regard, Green (2003) makes a case for the value of different perspectives and their integration. Applied to sexuality, it appears there has been a shift from biological to relational reductionism that limits the complexity of experience. Thus the drive, instinctual, biological components of sexuality need renewed recognition, and the concept of expansion needs ascendancy over alternative explanations.

WHAT IS SEXUALITY?

We have been talking about sexuality as though its meaning was clear and definition was not needed. In one sense, that is true because it does mean something to everybody, but not the same thing, which is a complication. Some explanation is required. Daniluk (1998) indicates that the most basic view of sex is anatomical, based on genitality at birth. Having sex, however, usually refers to some bodily contact, ranging from intercourse to masturbation. Sexuality covers the broader ground of anything related to sex, including erotic excitement, fantasy, and activity. Sexuality is what you make it. Each person constructs a personal version of what is considered sexual for that person. The numerous forms of sexuality are shaped by body potentials, environmental realities, cultural factors, and fantasy. So there is an ongoing selectivity and differentiation (Weeks, 1995).

A common factor in sexuality is the sensation of excitement, a physiological arousal that can be measured in terms of energy and is customarily experienced as some type of pleasurable bodily tension. The experience is often described as "feeling sexual." It may be accompanied by ideation and action, or it may not be accompanied by either. The causes of the excitement can be difficult to delineate, but appear to be bodily based. Defining sexual stimuli is an individual issue. It is possible to establish what is usually considered sexual, but that is not universal. There are significant numbers of behaviors that are considered unusual and sexual, such as fetishes, and there are people who resist the notion of their sexuality having to be gendered, as well as great differences in the degree of sexuality all people experience, Sexuality can be intimate, relational, an expression of love for another, and none of those. It can be part of another act, as hostility, or incorporate that act as part of sexual expression.

Feeling sexual usually motivates sexual action with the self or others. Included in the action is the maintenance or building of the excitement, and the aim is pleasure or satisfaction. Orgasm is not essential . Sexuality often serves as symbolic expression of a motive or feeling, such as unity. Sexuality can be experienced as an extreme form of intimacy ("I have never felt so close to anyone') or distance ('I felt nothing").

Sexuality has the potential for interweaving drives and connections amidst biological and cultural contexts. A person can feel as if they are another person. Or they can basically lose their partner. Sex can glorify the self, or focus on being selfless. There are too many varieties to offer an inclusive schema.

For the analyst, sexuality is what the patient describes, and what your experience is in relating to the patient. The material usually fits a variety of interpretive schemes. Some are customary, as Freud's approach as well as its modifications, some are relatively unusual, as Lacan's view that sexuality is essentially a linguistic exercise demonstrated in transference, an effect of signification involving a quest for specific meanings (Grosz, 1999). The process of discovery, the expression of desire, lies ahead.

In our concern for the restitution of the drive, instinct, impulse aspect of sexuality we are trying to refashion the dominance of a relational context for sexuality. This means rebalancing those approaches, as well as involving others. Admittedly this is a complex proposition, with plenty of room for disputes, but we see it as necessary to ensure the recognition of the importance of sexuality, and we accept the probability of sexuality being unable to fit with any concise model. Experience argues against any neat embrace, but the theoretical struggles need to continue because the matter is far from settled.

Reductionism in motivational systems has always had an appeal, and libido was the major offering in Freud's drive theory. Relational theory has had a lot of success in apparently developing further simplification regarding sexuality as well as proposing a broad umbrella for behavior that was not so well explained in drive theories. Approaches broadening motivational possibilities, as the hierarchy of motivations proposed by Pine (1990), the expansion of ego functions suggested by Blanck and Blanck (1994), and the five major motivations proposed by Lichtenberg (1989) foundered on the shoals of complexity when compared with reductionistic approaches. Duality theory got a bad name, one-person psychology, while the single motivations, relations, attachment, and connection, came into favor as two-person psychologies. Patients got proud as they realized they had been discovered in a way that was more appealing than the past, and analysts got humbled, or at least, so they professed.

Nonetheless, in recently attempting to develop a paradigm shift for aggression (Rizzuto, et al., 2004), the emphasis is on aggression as a motive, as well as on the context of motivation, stimuli, revised metapsychology, and the self as an agent. Essentially this is a broad theory of motivation reflective of the clinical experience of aggression. Beyond that, it is a way of stating that the existing alternatives are insufficient, akin to the possibilities for explaining sexuality.

We will not offer the same specifics, but we agree with the idea of expansion. Elsewhere (Herron, 1999) the point has been made that while all the major motivational possibilities can be shown to have value some of the time, their restrictive tendencies get in the way of fully explaining certain behaviors. In this case, sexuality has not been adequately represented. Sexuality is better explained by using parts of a number of existing approaches to motivation, as well as being inventive, to attempt to form an integrated comprehensive theory. We start with the impression that people have an inherent motivational potential toward self-organization. This includes the ordering of components of current prevalent theories of motivation in an individualized hierarchical manner (Pine, 1990). Motivation is then viewed as a structural organization of needs, desires and affects with a broad range. Sexuality is a major component, a strong motivational force of its own as well as being fed by a variety of other forces as instincts and connections to others. Rather than breaking down as it is examined, sexuality expands, becoming more complex.

The aim is pleasure, but the individual's perspective determines what constitutes sexual pleasure, or any other type of pleasure derived from activity considered sexual. Although sexuality aims to bring pleasure to the self and to others, it has suffered from numerous cultural prohibitions and taboos. The development of sexuality is often fraught with social problems that, in turn, become personalized. Society appears afraid of sexuality, despite its relatively benign nature. This seems paradoxical because if one is indeed concerned about "the beast within," or "man as animal," aggression is a far greater threat. Freud included an aggressive component in sexual intercourse as adding to the excitement, but when too intense became more a manifestation of sadistic or masochistic element. The harm we do to each other is rarely the result of sexual activity and frequently the result of hostility, but even in more enlightened times there remains considerable sexual guilt and social suppression. Anything other than ordinary male-female sexual intercourse is treated with some suspicion. The more behavior strays from this norm, the more it is likely to be considered deviant and pathological. We suspect it is the personal meanings attached to the polymorphous possibilities in sexuality that make people so selective, and fanatical, about what should be considered acceptable, non-perverted sexuality. At the same time, minority voices are speaking out and gaining interest in their views, so there is hope that the idea of sexuality as involving many acceptable variable patterns is closer to reality.

CONCLUSIONS

The shift in primary models of motivation from drive to relational has resulted in a lack of sufficient emphasis on the role of sexuality. Without depreciating the value of relational concerns, the instinctual aspect of sexuality needs reconsideration to fully account for patients' sexual experiences. Although sexuality is difficult to define because it is usually described in terms of personal meanings that have considerable variations, these descriptions carry affective drive and relational qualities. Sexuality is a complex concept that does not fit smoothly into a reductionistic approach to motivation. A more comprehensive model is needed. This seems possible by combining aspects of various other models, including drive and relational, as well as being open to new concepts.

People are motivated to organize themselves in response to their perceived importance of their needs. Thus a personal perspective develops that includes sexual excitement and expression. Each person is motivated to satisfy their needs, and each person has a variable inherent capacity to do this. An example is the concept of foreground and background in sexual expression with a variable dominance of sexual positions (Kassof, 2004) and the latter representing for us an instinctual component. The development of motivation and need-satisfaction is also influenced by external factors, as interpersonal relations, social, cultural, and ethnic factors. Sexuality is a part of the self with both internal and external components, capable of both a self-focus and interaction with others, of responding to unconscious and conscious stimuli, and to internal and external stimulation. What is considered sexuality is very much a matter of individual preference. Even when it is a matter of relatively general agreement that some situation is sexual, as in advertising for example, the reaction by different people will be contextual. Not everyone will agree, and the same holds true for situations that are supposedly not sexual. Freud made the point that sexuality is very much a personal matter when he originally expanded what could be considered libidinal.

The result is that sexuality is a very complex construct that engenders a large amount of confusion and distortion. Neglect of any of its components, whether instinctual or relational, restricts understanding the experience. The experience also is often understood by another as a co-construction, changing it somewhat from the experience itself when it is narrated, and its affective component is restricted in description by the need to use language. Simplifications of sexual motivation also have a containing flavor. The experience is potentially more expansive, more intricate, more powerful, and more mysterious than it has usually been depicted.

Chapter 2

GENDER ROLES

WHO AM I?

Perhaps it should be, what am I, boy, girl, or some other gendered being, although in this case the "what" is a "who, "the reference being to a person. Introducing his psychoanalytic theory of sexual development, which included sexual identity, Freud paid little attention to the question. He treated it as a biological given. You are who biology says you are, the initial coupling of biology and destiny that would be retained and expanded as a person's life unfolded, Freud was aware that there could be exceptions to the either-or rule, saw them as un frequent and problematic. This remains true as Money (1999) has noted in documenting variations that do occur, as hermaphroditism. Thus Freud put forth a theory of normal sexual development that treated anything else as a perversion. Then Stoller (1985) has added biological sexual disorders, such as defects of the sex chromosomes, of the genes, or prenatal conditions that are iatrogenic. These result in an apparent either-or that appears customary, but is not in terms of potential effects on the brain. The results are uncertainties in gender identity that seem to be particularly influenced by the person's biology, though it is not equivalent to biological determinism.

Freud may not have addressed the presence of biological exceptions at birth because they were rare and most likely would result in identity confusion that would be unusual. He was focused on how sexuality usually developed, and in particular, on the effects of repression, social, personal, and parental, in creating neuroses. He did not view the person as system of self-differentiated from others until some time after birth. So a gendered self as a dualism, or even a significant difference was not much of. a consideration. The timing of the existence of a gender identity, other than nominally, depends on when the sense of self is postulated to exist as distinct, as well as the formation of self-representations and object-representations. A key question is whether the infant is moving from less to greater differentiation in regard to inside-outside, self-other, or the reverse, or moving one way in certain areas, such as differentiation of affects, and a different way in others, as object relations.

The controversy has been primarily about the dualism of separation individuation as opposed to growth-in-connection. Separation originated with Freud and was neatly elaborated to match psychosexual and psychosocial stages by Mahler, Bergman, and Pine (1975), as contrasted with connection theory, building on the work of Stern (1985) and most forcibly depicted by Miller (1976).

The earlier the sense of a self that recognizes the other, the earlier the sense of a gendered self, even without an awareness of genital differences. Freud saw that issue as being particularly tied to the Oedipal situation. Prior to that a person's gender identity was based on what they had been told at birth based 'on their anatomy. Even if a differentiated self exists at birth, making a connection between gender and anatomy is improbable without input from others. It is these others who usually make the connection for the person, and often without much of an anatomical explanation, or without creating an understanding of that distinction. Even when children have body awareness, it is limited, and their view of gender is mainly based on what they have been told. Gender begins as a taught concept. The significance of the penis and the vagina develop more gradually, despite in one-way being the bedrock of gender identity.

The obvious superficial characteristics of boy-girl are embraced more readily, even though many of these can be changed readily, as hair, clothes, mannerisms, and attitudes. In contrast, genital anatomy is the defining characteristic that is kept under wraps, to the point that for some time each gender is aware of their own genitals without necessarily having an awareness of differences. Gender identity originates primarily as a social construct that involves the body, but often is not based on a self-awareness of major anatomical structural defining characteristics.

In one sense gender identity refers to the personal sense of being male or female, regardless of anatomical distinctions. However, there is also the identity issue of having male or female genitals and living in accord with the social roles prescribed for those genitals. Stoller (1985) views gender identity as a mixture of masculinity and femininity, with these being beliefs as to what is masculine or feminine. This is a reflection of Freud's belief in the inborn potential for bisexuality that is limited not so much by anatomy as by social and cultural influences.

Freud believed the sense of one's gender identity became more self-apparent with an awareness of actual genital differences and the passage through the Oedipal stage. In the preoedipal years, boys and girls were viewed as rather similar, with a bias toward the value of masculinity for everybody. Little emphasis was given directly to a gendered self, male and female roles, or object relations. The psychosocial was relatively neglected in favor of the psychosexual, although ego psychology did redress that markedly with the stages of separation-individuation. However, even there the sense of sexual identity was not highlighted. In a slight expansion, the anatomy-destiny link came to mean something more than anatomy provides certain potentials, genetic, hormonal, and brain, that to varying degrees differentiate males from females. Instead, it was thought that penis and vagina pointed the way and progressively determined that the self be masculine or feminine. Normal sexuality stayed an either-or proposition, with variations considered pathological. There was not much elasticity in the theory.

Basic Gender Identity

In a variation on preceding views of psychosexual development, Stoller (1985) suggested the development of a core gender identity was an initial step. This consisted of a conviction that one's assigned sex was both psychologically and anatomically correct. He believed this developed between 2-3 years of age and was relatively fixed. Recent evidence suggests this was incorrect, sexuality being capable of fluidity over each person's life (DeCecco & Parker, 1995), but that doe not negate the possibility of the original formation of a core gender identity. What is called into question is the degree of conviction one has, or keeps, about it. The question of who I am has a self-developed answer, but not an invariant one. This is most apparent in people with ambiguous sexual anatomy who in turn have a very contingent sexuality. It is also true for people who self-identify in ways that are not customary for a masculine or feminine gender identity. This gender identity usually comes about, as part of overall identity that includes a variety of recognitions, such as my name is Mary, and that is a girl's name, so I am a girl. Gender identity is not basic to an awareness of sexuality because sexual excitement is potentially gender-neutral, open to whatever sexual choice is available and appealing. However, gender identity becomes intertwined with sexual preference and object choice, considerations for the next chapter.

Stoller suggests core gender identity is formed by a number of factors, including a genetic biological force connected to brain organization, sex assignment at birth coupled with parental attitudes and handling, and genital sensations. Our impression is that while all these factors can be considered as contributors to gender identity, the discernment of being male, female, or something else, requires knowledge associated with these categories as well as their corresponding anatomical correlates. Thus gender selectivity takes place over time and is potentially flexible. The original bisexuality, or really pansexuality, is essentially modified to meet developing sexual appetites.

Gender identity is closely connected to sexual preference and the concept of identification. Freud centered gender identity on possession and power, which he saw as masculine attributes. At the same time he postulated instinctual bisexuality, but with the idea of feminine inferiority and passivity. Bisexuality was not considered sexual equality. Instead the model was androcentric where boys learn that they have something girls don't have, a penis, which is considered a more visible and pleasurable organ. Of course the concept can be reversed, as a number of women analysts have pointed out. Girls could take pride in having a vagina and enjoying their genital sensations. The visibility of the penis can be a hardship in terms of physical vulnerability and just plain getting in the way. Thus, designation of feminity as a deprivation based on the absence of a penis is a reversible position. Each gender can make the best of what they have without any essential inferiority or superiority.

Fast (1984) approaches the issue in terms of loss of over inclusiveness. The developing self is seen as initially unaware of the differences between what a boy and girl can do. Elise (1997) describes a period when the self-representation first discovers limits, then moves on to the effects of such limits, which are tied to gender identity. There is the possibility of loss, the specifics depending on one's fantasies and applicable to males and females, both of whom were likely to have an exaggerated view of what they thought they could do. The recognition of gender identity does not have to be connected to limits on object choices (Herron, 1999).

Another issue is identification with the primary caretaker. This has tended to be viewed in a very literal manner. Because the mother is usually the most frequent caretaker, both boys and girls have been described as identifying with her. Because she is a woman the assumption is made that girls have an obvious identification, same genitals as well as some other similarities, but identification rests on more than just that type of gender identity. In fact, it may have much more to do with the caretaker's nurturing qualities than who or who does not have a vagina or a penis. Attachment theory lends support to the formation of connections and identifications with caretakers who appear to provide the greatest security. The desire for a good mother and forming an identification with whoever your mother is do not necessarily go together. When children attach themselves to bad mothers and adults to bad objects, there is an identification with a projected concept that the person believes is essential for survival. This becomes more a matter of perceived self-survival than anatomy or frequency of contact, though these can be contributing influences.

A girl may simply become aware that both she and her mother are female, so that becomes her gender identity. The boy can make that identification with the father even if the father is not the major caretaker. The qualities identified with in a parent, however, are not necessarily the qualities of the same-gendered parent. Instead the child's self is organized around a concept of being male or female that is adaptive for the child. Gender identity is partially an identification with the reality of anatomy as well as the parental and social designations corresponding to anatomical awareness, and partially a set of attributes that the self finds appealing. The infant becomes gendered as the child, then the adolescent, and then the adult who both self-identifies and is identified by others in reaction to the self-identity. The person then displays the attributes of that gender based both on personal and cultural impressions.

When there are anatomical variations, then there is confusion. People in that situation make choices for their gender, usually male or female, but at times some variation for which there is no neat categorization. Psychological identity is associated with physical gender identity, but does not have to correspond to the anatomical designation. Sometimes gendered males or females choose to change their anatomy and identity to correspond, where other times the change is only in psychological identity. So there are transsexuals, intersexuals, hermaphrodites, transvestites, gays, and lesbians. Some of this categorization mixes anatomy and attributes considered masculine or feminine, and some relies primarily on appearing to be masculine or feminine.

Gender identity is ultimately a personal matter, although some physical characteristics appear as a better fit with anatomical gender than cross gendering. However, regardless of initial design, if personal feelings and preferences are not in alignment with that design, conflict occurs. Anatomical gender is actually only a preliminary plan, subject to powerful social-cultural-relational influences that can change the initial design. Anatomy can be destiny, but is not an automatic determiner of object choice. The instinctual component is sexuality in general, not gendered sexuality aligned with masculinity or femininity. These are social-political constructions that are often depicted as "natural" to disguise their true origins.

Masculine and Feminine

Psychoanalysis was founded by a man and mainly developed by men using a model that supported the superiority of men, which could raise some questions as to its revolutionary aspects. Of course it was also a cultural product, and still is. The radical aspects lay in its challenge to prevalent sexual beliefs, which also opened the theory to pose challenges to its original phallocentric model. If bisexuality had prevailed as a potential free from a predestined choice based supposedly on biology, then the theory could have postulated the freedom of all individuals to choose their own ways of being masculine or feminine, or a "third' for the minorities that need a solution other than being a male or female.

Instead, either-or dualism has dominated. Femininity has been very useful in highlighting positive qualities that are considered feminine, but given the prevailing bias of the past, a lot of time has also been spent on depreciating masculinity. The result is that a connection is made between relational theory and femininity in contrast to what is often considered a more masculine structural theory. This is a reflection of a bias in each theory regarding motivation, as well as a false sense of determinism for masculinity and femininity. O'Neil, Good, and Holmes (1995) provide an extensive review of what society tends to view as masculine, and Enns (2000) does the same for femininity. In psychoanalysis, the penis has been the prize, a symbol of power possessed by men due to biology. Women have too often been depicted as being inferior to men and wanting to be men. Culturally, the " true male" is aggressive, autonomous, and in control. He is the emotionally detached, all-knowing analyst of the foibles of others, particularly women. This gender identity of the warrior male was long considered the appropriate outcome of anatomical gender, modified adaptively by ego and superego to essentially civilize sexuality and aggression.

Of course psychoanalysis has as its core the idea of revelation for all genders, which opens up a paradox in any attempts to maintain a patriarchic view of the world. Also, the relational movement, which was prominently engendered by men, provides additional fuel for the incompleteness of making penis envy and castration fears central factors in determining gender roles. There just isn't support for the universal naturalness of gender roles. Whatever way women and men may be disposed by their biology is potentially variant. While we believe it is very important to give considerable weight to the instinctual component of sexuality, masculine and feminine gender roles are primarily social constructions. They are influenced by biology, but not inevitably determined by it.

INFANT RESEARCH

People seem to be born with innate self-organizations and sexual instincts. At birth, these are immature, varying and developing over the life span. We have noted that the concept of a sexual instinct originates in the earliest forms of psychoanalytic theorizing. It now requires revitalization because of contemporary challenges to the notion of drive that have tended to desexualize the self.

The idea of a differentiated self at birth, with possible prenatal antecedents (Herron,1999), is in contrast to early psychoanalytic theory, which emphasized a lack of differentiation. It also differs from the customary psychosocial stages. These do propose a strong tendency toward relating, but begin with infantile autism and symbiosis preceding awareness of others outside the self. Lyons-Ruth (1991) has suggested that research on early relationships indicates that what was originally called separation individuation, is more accurately described as attachment-individuation. This view emphasizes relatedness as an innate capacity. Contact-avoidance is an issue in establishing desired attachments.

The works of Stern (1985) and of Sander (1985) have been particularly influential in illustrating the presence of an early organizing self that from birth uses inner experience as well as interactions with the outside world. Beebe and Lachmann (2002) present an extensive review of infant research supporting the view that the infant is born with complex organizational skills that are quickly developed within interactional contexts. While we lean toward a more inherent organization of the self in its inception, our views are congruent with an ongoing co-construction of the developing experience. This early differentiation, as well as the interest in attachment, and the potential for the formation of mutual systems, support this idea that the child learns gender identity as well as the gender role that is to be enacted. Although sexuality has biological and psychosocial components that are influential, sexuality is not reducible to a single component. In summarizing the research evidence, Parker and DeCecco state, "...sexuality is a biological, emotional, psychological, and social experience for each of us " (1995. p.430).

An intriguing question persists. Why does each person define their sexual identity in a particular way? Here psychoanalytic theory has to be open to all possible influences in each personal history. The search for explanatory markers is intriguing, and the possibility of discovery is appealing in terms of fostering the understanding of behavior, but the results so far have not been particularly helpful. Exceptions continually appear, so whatever guidelines gain some credence, they need to be understood as only some possibilities among many, with an untold number of others yet to be discovered, and some behaviors retaining a mysterious etiology. We believe there are explanations to all sexual behaviors, but often do not know exactly what they are. That is the norm, rather than the exception, but a great deal can be discovered about a person's sexuality that is of both interest and value, so the exploration continues.

In particular, it is disturbing to see the results of the insistence on normalizing heterosexual intercourse while pathologizing so much of the rest of sexuality, if for no other reason than pathology can also be found in heterosexual intercourse. What we are looking is for an opening of the inquiry to allow multiple possibilities that are more in keeping with the observed experience. We understand that the assumption of any gender role identity can be defensive as a reaction to some disturbing affect, and that is important to understand when that is happening. However, that is vastly different from the widespread theories and beliefs that foster one type of sexual behavior really on the grounds of personal preference and social pressure. The enormous value judgments that have gone on have both been erroneous in many instances as well as harming people.

We also recognize that sexuality can be used for harmful purposes, as rape, pedophilia, and incest, and that such behavior is pathological. The same term can be applied to personal sexual behavior that restricts sexuality in a way that is disturbing to the self or others, as premature ejaculation, erectile dysfunction, and inability to have orgasms. Such situations emphasize the continuing need to understand sexuality and develop remedies when problems do exist.

Understanding personal sexual history is the best key to explaining the manner in which people enact their sexual identities. It is helpful to eliminate the idea of inevitable direct links between biological and psychological factors and behavior. These factors are more likely to be correlates. Causes are more likely to be multiple and to result in indirect, confusing, and variable routes to behavior that retains a fluid potential. Also, the influence of social, ethnic, cultural, and atmospheric factors needs greater acknowledgement.

For example, a male-gendered child will identify with his father in the sense that he considers himself a biological male, and the same is true for a girl and her mother, but that does not explain the feelings about the identifications, nor does it indicate what a male or female will do with their given gender. Gender role provides opportunities and limitations. For example, a male is likely to be able to impregnate females, but cannot get pregnant. Social norms have provided males with greater chances for financial success. Traditional feminine ways, as submission, can restrict male success. Women are often suspect in terms of their mental toughness and competitiveness. Biological and social gender roles are often intertwined and limited in their validity, but have considerable impact. Identifying as male or female does not require the assumption of superiority of either matriarchy or patriarchy as a life style. A person needs to be able to integrate gender identity with the adaptive use of personal sexuality. How that is being accomplished, as well as the obstacles, are explored in the next chapter.

Some clinical examples are useful at this point to further illustrate the concerns just raised around the manner of displaying being male or female.

A gay man mentions, "You know, not that many people know I am gay. I mean, gay people can tell, a gay man knows another one, but the rest, they can't tell unless you act gay."

"And you don't?"

"I don't think I do, I mean not in the way straights imagine gays to be, you know, feminine."

"I'm hesitant to assure you that I do know. Because, you see my idea of what is feminine and yours, they could be different."

"Sure, but some gays, the way they walk, talk, dress even, and I don't mean in drag, but it is just there. If you saw it, you would know it."

"Could I, could both of us, be wrong in some cases, you know, just from observing?"

"I suppose."

"But, not likely?"

"Right."

This man was convinced that there are definite ways to appear masculine or feminine that are socially convincing. He was also sure that gay people can take on a "disguise" when necessary, and he believed he had done this. As the notorious Frank Costello is reported to have said, "Tough guys don't dance." This is just one of the many examples that could be cited of male and female stereotypes. They are relatively common and influential. However, the existence of masculine and feminine types does not necessarily reveal the totality of gender role identity. They do have considerable importance in developing a desired image, but are not as convincingly acquired as the patient believed. Although he had come to the analyst with phobic anxiety, the analyst viewed him as "somewhat feminine," and in turn wondered, if at some point, the patient would say he was gay. The analyst was aware of the subjectivity of the perception of masculinity, and that he was associating the perception of femininity in a man with gayness, which could be an error. In this case the analyst's association was correct. At the same time, the patient had a strong need to feel that he looked straight to most people, but it was quite probable that he did not, so his belief was incorrect. The possible confusion available is striking.

The patient's feelings were about the possible connection of femininity with gayness, and a concern that if some people in his world also made this connection because they actually did see him as feminine, he would be derided in some way. This was certainly a possibility. In a protective response to such a happening, he decided that he could be gay and appear to be straight if he wished. He based his belief on the fact that people said nothing to him that would suggest they thought he was gay. The analyst's guess was that he was not deceiving people based on stereotypical appearance, but that he was an appealing person whose sexual orientation was of little concern to the people around him. In essence, it can be tough to look tough, or meet many appearance stereotypes, but the importance of this issue is by no means an absolute. However, it is clear that how this man believed he looked, and the potential meaning he associated to his appearance, was a big concern to him. In turn, that made an issue out of the possible components of masculinity, which occurs frequently for femininity as well.

In another instance a woman said to her analyst, "Sometimes I just do not appear to be feminine, I'm afraid. I mean, it makes me wonder, does that turn guys off?"

"Could you tell me more about this?"

"I ask myself, am I gay? But I am not interested in women that way. In fact I even like the company of men better than I like being with women."

"In that regard, about being gay, you have told me that you have had a number of opportunities for lesbian encounters, but you did not take them."

"No, I didn't, because I don't find women appealing as sexual partners. I wish I did. I think I would attract more people."

"Because you think you look like a lesbian?"

"Yes."

"In this case you mean looking masculine rather than feminine?"

"Yes. Well, I suppose it all goes together, the looks, the actions, but more than the looks, I think I act masculine."

"Well, what if you do?"

"Men don't like that. It isn't how women act."

"You want to change that?"

"Does that mean you think I act like a man?"

"It means you told me that is how you feel you act, and that you feel there is something wrong with this way. You also seem to have some uncertainty about whether you act in this manner, but seem mainly convinced you do, and that it could be driving men away from you, men you want to attract."

"I do wish I was more feminine. My mother was not, and I am not, although I really do feel I am a woman. My body tells me I am a woman, and so does my mind in many ways, but sometimes, I don't know, I think I act like I am one of the guys."

"I sense the conflict you are in, and it probably is increased because your job is technical and you are considered very capable. So you have the power of a man. You know this stuff should not bother, would not bother, many men."

"I know it as a theory, but I feel like nobody wants me because I am too much like a man. I have had to be assertive to get where I am, and now it is messing me up."

"You may scare some men, but let's go back to the other parts of this, that you feel you are not feminine enough."

"You mean looks, style?"

"Yes. The way I hear it you are saying that you are the feminine equivalent of the man who feels he is not masculine enough, and he is not gay."

"That is pretty much it. I feel as if I come across as some kind of masculine woman who, on that basis, could be mistaken for a lesbian, but who is not. This masculinity of mine attracts some lesbians and turns off most men. So it shouldn't be that way, but I think it really is. Something is really off."

Something is off all right, but not primarily with the patient, although she has the problem, and the need to solve it. The people who conform to the more usual aspects of a gender role identity have an easier time of developing a cohesive self. All the parts come to them. For others, they are considered not masculine or feminine enough to easily enact their gender role identities. As a result, they have to struggle to attract people from a smaller group, namely those who do not care about relatively superficial issues, or who are actually attracted by the very traits that people feel will drive others away.

In the case of this woman, the analyst could see how she drew her conclusions, and did not disagree as to what might be happening. However, the analyst experienced her as feminine. Her anxiety, which was palpable, seemed more of a problem, but as in the previous example, the desire to fit a role eluded the patient and that was disturbing. In contrast to the previous example, where the man thought he could successfully assume a role that felt false but necessary, as well as accessible, the woman felt she could not assume a role that felt real. The role felt elusive and the same time she believed it ought to belong to her.

In each situation, ideally, the essence and identity of the person had the potential to be palliative, but involved issues of perceived masculinity and femininity, which hindered a healing, process. These cases emphasize that the analyst has to consider not only intrapsychic and relational issues, but the reality of social and cultural factors.

Chapter 3

Gender Preference

Sticks and Stones

In the case of whom do you prefer, man, woman, or whomever comes along, names can hurt you. Heterosexual preferences are expected. Same-sex choice brings the names, and the names can bring the blows, psychic and physical. This situation has a long history, preceding psychoanalysis, and Lacan, who with his emphasis on signification, forged a strong link between sexuality and language. Now there are numerous efforts to get just the right word, or phrase, to describe people's sexuality, and these efforts include disagreements within the groups that are expending most of the efforts.

For example, Butler (1993) offers the lesbian phallus as a symbolic expression of female power and competence. Although agreeing with the idea of a female body symbol of power, this one seems too phallic for Roth (2004), who instead suggests the lesbian clitoris. Both of these phrases are a bit difficult, so we would pick clitoris, without a modifier, although Roth sketches the history of how metaphorically the clitoris shrank as the phallus grew.

Language inscription has been a strong determinant of the roles and attributes of both men and women, with men traditionally winning the word war, which in turn, has tended to be a world war. Although there are cultures that do not facilitate the ascendancy of heterosexuality and binary gender (Francoeur & Noonan, 2004), they are exceptions to mainstream cultural sexuality. The use of a new language as a frequent means of signification is most likely to be a long struggle, accompanied by rejections of both the new and the old.

For example, should we have called this chapter, "orientation," rather than, "preference?" We used "preference," because we think of sexuality as a cluster of appealing behaviors and fantasies for which we have a preference. The reason the word could be an issue is because preference suggests choice, whereas orientation does not, which is still another issue to be considered later. It is not, however, the issue we were considering in our word choice.

After that unexpected psychic confusion, let us get away from word usage and into sexuality, although we do hear Lacan laughing at the thought that such disconnection is either possible or plausible. Scaer (2001) emphasizes the centrality of sexuality in personal identity. Thus, using one word rather than another can, indeed, say something about who we are. However, the subjective motivations for the word usage are not so transparent. We often use words that fit our historical experience, as "male" and "female," as our knowledge code, but consider that these terms are not equivalent to the totality of the person, nor do they imply universality of features resulting from genetic construction. We use the boxes of familiarity as containers, but are always attempting to think outside of those boxes, as well as within them. In order for marginality to be reduced, men's errors do not have to be repeated by women, nor do heterosexual distortions have to infiltrate the gay community. We are bound to use words at times that will seem disturbing to some, incorrect to others, and Lacan would probably say that is because we are caught up in the lack that is desire, and in term we are being sexual. Nonetheless, we ask that you keep your eye on our stated intentions. We are trying to develop an improved psychoanalytic theory of sexuality. Where we sense new words and terms are needed, we will use them, and where we do not, we will not, but that does not rule out reinterpretation of the past; after all, Lacan built a substantial reputation from reworking Freud.

Of course, they were both misunderstood people, which is very useful in keeping a theory alive. For example, every time we think we have Freud in our knowledge pockets, someone urges us to read his footnotes. As for Lacan, he might have said "phallus," but may not have literally meant "penis." Instead, it does seem something imaginary was on his mind. Actually, we have a sense that the phallus gets manhandled by Lacan, and woman handled by Butler, but we hope these are misconceptions. The phallus as penis, which is familiar usage to so many of us, does not usually resemble an erect building toppled only by the strongest of forces. Ironically, the power of the phallus is more of a myth than the pull of the vagina, which is probably why men have worked so hard to keep phallocentrism alive.

That brings us to "queer theory," which along with feminism and relational emphases, works against the biological essentialism of binary gender, as well as its social construction. The term, "queer," plays on the paradox of pejorative naming by embracing all sexual orientations and forming links with feminism and relational theory. Their view is that we are all the same in that we are cultural gender products, so in that sense, regardless of sexual preferences or orientations, there is universal queerness. A person might usually be considered marginal based on sexual behavior, but with queer as normal, marginality is reduced. However, it does not appear to be eliminated, because although queer theory embraces a much wider group of sexualities as normative, it appears primarily focused on homosexuality, heterosexuality, and bisexuality. Apparently excluded are more unusual sexual expressions, as necrophilia, pedophilia, extremes of sadism and masochism,and whatever else that could be listed as both sexual and very likely to be considered pathological by people other than those doing it. The end result is that queer has limits as to what is normative, but the limits are less restrictive than those present in other theories considered to be significant.

In attempting to develop viable ways of depicting sexuality, words are a problem. So are differences that pose threats to an established social system that satisfies enough people to keep it relatively intact throughout most of the world. However, the system is creaking. The International Psychoanalytic Association recently put in place an official nondiscrimination policy regarding homosexuals (Roughton, 2003), and Linqiardi and Drescher (2003) show how progress has been made internationally in depathologizing homosexuality. There is little to fear from being queer, except the anxiety of the reality of any person's sexual possibilities. Apparently, that is a very strong anxiety.

Such anxiety makes all theories vulnerable to problems, and to exclusions. Some aspects of sexuality may well need to be marginalized and do need to be controlled because of their destructive potential. At the same time, the control principle has been subject to devastating overkill, prompting the emergence of an approach such as queer theory. For example, rape fantasies and playing rape games might make it into queer territory, but rape will not because lines have to be drawn regarding sexual acceptability. This is, indeed, a complex issue, because even the example we just used, rape, which we are considering to be a violent sexual act, could be thought of by some queer theorists as violence rather than sex, and so not open to our categorization. However, if accepted as a sexual act, rape easily makes the point that you have to have limits in terms of sexual freedom, but other sexual behaviors are more difficult to classify as in or out, pathological or acceptable. For example, who is harmed in necrophilia? Nonetheless, the motivation has to be discovered and explored. Is this acceptable sex, or is it deviant? Is it a manifestation of a psychic problem? Most people would probably say it was a disorder, necrophiliacs being a small and rather quiet voice among the marginalized. We admit to finding necrophilia "creepy," as though there has to be something wrong with it. It is not consensual, so that's a start.

The major point here is that a lot of unusual behavior gets entangled in sexuality, and disentangling what is problematic from what is not, is a monumental task. It is really beyond our capacities on a general basis, so it has to be carried out on a specific basis. This means detailed consideration of all the behavior and people involved. The aim is to develop sufficient supporting evidence to make a relatively definitive judgment, but that cannot always occur. Rather than attempt a diagnostic schema for sexuality, we will continue our efforts on the broadening of the range of normative sexual possibilities and the normalcy of sexual excitement (Herron. 1999).

Why Gender Matters

The waves of deconstructionism wash away much of what was familiar, what was supposedly known, what was even considered certainty. Deconstructing gender has changed the concepts of man and woman, and the subjectivities attached to these concepts. In particular, the idea of being bound by maleness or femaleness to particular roles, as well as to particular ways of thinking and feeling, has been radically altered for many people, although by no means everyone. The changes are more prevalent among people identified with a white Eurocentric culture than for people of color where class and ethnicity are more powerful modifying variables (Collins, 2000; Segura, 2001).

Regardless of these changes, sexuality retains a central place in identity formation and development, and gender is a strong indicator of the possibilities and limitations of sexuality. It is a starting point for all of us, the opening to a potential for whatever degree of gender bending is going to occur. Thus, within deconstruction there remains a value in knowing the steps involved in constructing gender identity.

For Freud (1905, 1914), gender and relationships were about the loss of primary narcissism in a necessary movement to secondary narcissism that was costly as it involved the intrusion of the ego and superego into the id. He viewed the self as originating in an undifferentiated way that maintained omnipotence (my voice is my command) and an objectless self (I am because I am). Reality at some point broke down this illusion, deconstructed it one might say. This change was experienced as a loss of omnipotence rather than a gain of an object world. Attachment patterns, relationships, identifications, and object choices all happened, but not due to a desire for these events. Instead, as differentiation unfolded, they became necessary.

In the novel, *Straight Man*, one of the female characters states, "Love doesn't require an object. It's like clouds. When you're flying through them. You're just in them, and then you're not" (Russo, 1997, p. 350).

There it is, still around, objectless libido. The original drive was not about people, but about being in a state. Freud recognized that libido could and would be satisfied through others, but love was given to others to get their love, which in turn served as the food for secondary narcissism. Self-esteem was depleted by loving, but restored by being loved. People did not need other people to love primarily, but people love others so these people will love them and allow them to go on being in love with themselves. Sublimations are there as safety valves, along with all the less successful defenses, in case of unrequited love, or unextended love for those who took no chances.

As love unfolded through the psychosexual stages, so did object relatedness, basically through the components of identification that resulted in genital primacy, self-identity, and object constancy. Gender identity formation was a key component of this process. Boys will be boys, and then men, and their libidinal desires will focus on both parents, and on boys and girls. The process again involves loss, now of the security that is threatened by castration fears in particular. In addition, as paternal identification takes place and becomes primary, there is some identity splitting in giving up some of the maternal identification. There is also a relatively specific type of penis envy, the desire for a bigger one, implying a loss of what might have been. All this combines in driving a shift away from parental objects and toward others and the outside world. The boy will become the man, incorporating his object choice, a female, and surrender homeoerotic desires to relatively desexualized affection. Most of this was considered to operate in the realm of the unconscious, but even with that possibility, a lot of it is not convincing. Sexual desire, at least some imitation of the father, and phallic interest, seem accurate, but the rest of it seems to be a social construction designed to support the established heterosexual order and family creation.

For example, the idea that a boy decides he is a potential man based on his own awareness of anatomical similarity to his father is not nearly as probable as the boy having been told that he is a potential man, like his father, and being treated that way by caretakers, peers, and society in general. His object choice is usually in the same category, a designated gender role, which of course only works if he finds that more attractive than some other sexual orientation. Queer theory is a reaction to the limitations imposed on gender roles.

Freud's attempts to explain girls becoming women was even stronger in the emphasis on loss, with both castration and penis envy seen as much closer to reality than being threats. Female inferiority was a basic feature, with some hope residing in having babies, as well as getting a penis now and then through sexual activity with men. Girls did have an easier job completing the process of same-sex identification because they would not have to give up women's customary object choices, men. Because both genders were likely to get more care taking from their mothers, this was viewed as promoting females as the most obvious target for libidinal desires, which would become more erotic and genital over time for both sexes. The boy could keep his father's object choice, a female, but would lose his identification with his mother, which by proximity and degree of attention was likely to be greater than his anatomical identification with his father.

A whole lot of switching going on, which is fascinating in its retrospective twists in logic. For example, the mothering person is usually female, and by virtue of being a mother, is highly desired as both an object of imitation and erotic interest. At the same time, by being a woman, she is essentially flawed. However, it takes a while for each gender to catch on to the flaws. The boy, fortunately for him, does not have to be like the mother, thereby escaping the basic problem of being a female. However, he does have to spend a lot of time chasing after an inferior being to satisfy his lust and produce progeny. Wacky setup one might conclude, and so indeed, many have, but reformulation has proven far more difficult than criticism.

FREUD'S BIOPSYCHOLOGY

Freud was the one who had both the courage and the brilliance to fashion an original theory of sexuality. He just did not expect to be deconstructed. The people he theorized about and worked with were gendered as social products of those times, but he only touched on a portion of the social influences. He aptly contested social restrictions and the blindness to childhood sexuality, as well as the neurotic effects of inhibited sexuality. He used a reshaped Oedipal myth to try to account for important processes, such as identification and selection of sexual partners, as well as understanding family structure. However, he could not successfully take the theory beyond heterosexual intercourse without pathologizing the rest of sexuality. Feminism was not in his repertoire, so sexual equality was not considered to be a normative possibility.

Freud viewed sexuality as a mix of biology and social construction, and that idea remains accurate. However, distortions appear in the way the ingredients were mixed. For example, women were considered inferior to men because of the lack of a penis. The more likely reason for women's inferior status was that men had the power, the society was patriarchal, and women were subjugated. So, where he could have based an explanation on social factors, or even on the aggressive drive in connection with the pleasure of male narcissism, he used anatomy instead. However, he was not consistent in a biological emphasis. When it came to explaining why boys and girls switch their sexual desires outside the family, he relied on an incest taboo, fear of punishment, and continued development of a society. Even giving these factors an evolutionary flavor, they fit social conventions representative of the superego, which has the least anatomical ties of the triumvirate.

Freud was developing a psychological theory with some biological underpinnings, but his approach often appeared to be more of a biopsychology than the reverse. His interest in social factors bordered on the incidental, so the influence of class and race were underplayed. That part is ironic because being a Jew could have gotten Freud killed, but he may have wanted to repress that fact, and he was always more interested in libido than aggression.

He took on the major task of explaining how people are born with diffuse sexuality and then turn it into gendered object choice most of the time, and usually the choice is of the opposite gender. Also, there are significant exceptions, now amply noted in queer theory and accepted in some psychoanalytic theories. He chose to frame those choices in evolutionary, biological terms primarily, with some psychology mixed in, as the transformation of libido into love, the concepts of castration anxiety and phallic envy, and the pleasure principle that combines energy discharge and affect. Above all, and this is why it is so difficult to classify his theory in regard to the somatic-psychic balance, he made an enormous fuss about meaning.

THEORETICAL CHALLENGES

Biological determinism has certainly come under critical pressure from women, beginning with early female analysts such as Karen Horney and Clara Thompson, both of whom saw the power difference in gender based primarily on cultural differences. This theme has been continued by cultural feminists as Miller, Gilligan, Belenky, Goldberger, Chodorow, and Jordan (Enns, 2004), who stressed the importance of relationships, the special capacities of women for empathy, affiliation, and nurturance, and viewed the failures of connections as the major cause of psychopathology. Their views tie in with relational theory in general as well as the empathic attunement concept of self-psychology.

These approaches are also mixtures of biology and culture. There is the assumption that women are naturally more connected than men, as well as the fact that women have been made to feel inferior by social forces. The view of relationships is quite different from Freud's, where people were essentially forced to relate and went reluctantly. In more contemporary approaches, relating is akin to a drive, and there is an emphasis on early interactions that presage desire for attachment, connection, and empathy. Sexual connections are under this umbrella, but the driving internal libidinal force is disputed. Desire and lust appear now to rest in combined attractions, outside to inside and back out again. People stimulate attraction that is present as an inherent potential for connection.

Relational models, as well as self-models, are congruent with Freud's concept of identification, though they are not as specific about this resulting in normative gendered roles and identities. When it comes to sexual preference, they embrace the possibility of multiplicity, but do not appear to offer a theory of how one gets where one arrives, or what is a developmental problem and what is not. Much is made of connections to others, particularly caretakers. However, while mothers might admit they raised their sons to be cowboys, they do not usually say they raised them to be gay. Most gay and lesbian patients that we have experienced report that their sexual orientation came about in spite of their parents' wishes for them, not because they were raised to be marginalized. An unsettled issue is what gay and lesbian parents want for their children, and how much influence they have. Our experience also suggests that parents will accept a variety of sexual orientations for their children, but do not want to foster their development unless they are in line with parents' expectations. Identification with opposite-sex preference remains the norm for parental and cultural encouragement, but clearly not all children follow that path, nor do all children follow the same preference as their parents. Even among those who do, not all are comfortable with the choice if they feel it has been forced upon them by others.

So, same-sex identification is not a neat model for sexual preferences. We believe in the multiplicity of sexual possibilities, but that does not answer the question of how any one possibility became the reality; of how sexual desire moved in one direction, but not in another. Despite the potential fluidity of sexuality, sexual preference tends to be fairly persistent, resulting in subjective designations that are relatively entrenched and have often been established by vigorous effort. Why this, why not that? A normative answer, such as Freud/s, and much of society's, is misplaced.

POSSIBILITIES AND PROBABILITIES

Dimen (2003) provides help with her description of contingency theory, which she neatly condenses into, "It all depends" (p.14). Yes, but, we ask, depends on what? She proceeds to tell us, it depends on a lot of things, almost anything one could say, many answers, lots of variability, all quite subjective.

That is intriguing, but we would like something more precise. Well, perhaps when it comes to sex, precision cannot be the order of the day. In addition, we have already endorsed messiness. Now, is it fair that we ask for precision? Not fair, but we have a need to know, and patients have a need to know. Psychoanalysis explores with the hope of finding answers, and in the process accepts many unknowns. In this case, we want more than contingency that is so amorphous, so we will make a try for it. We also feel that patients want analysts to do just that, to keep trying to help them figure out how they became whomever it is they seem to be. Despite the fact that there is much more unknown than we know, or maybe because of that, and admitting to not knowing can be a virtuous as well as a brave act, though at times also foolhardy, we are on a quest for more knowledge here. The unconscious continues its work, because that sentence was contingency at work. Nonetheless, we want to know how people come to choose the gender of their sexual partners.

Kernberg (1976) suggested a model of introjection, identification, and ego identity. The person takes in, selectively, what is around and available, then imitates, also selectively, and emerges as a person with an "I." The surround begins with caretakers, probably mostly the mother, although there are variations on that, but let us call the major caretaker, mother. After that, models of identification proliferate, with multiculturalism showing there can be many mothers and more than one version of family. For example, campadrazgo in Chicano and other Latino families depicts relationships enlarging families as well as creating between-family connections. The path to identity is selective, influenced by personal proclivities whose origins may be unconscious, unknown, unsuspected, or knowable, with or without logical support, but powerful. It is also a function of class, status, privilege, race, gender, parental and peer pressure, and personal incentive. The recognition of the influence of all these factors, plus others we have failed to mention, is most likely to be incomplete, even in the most enduring of investigations, but a constellation of ideas about etiology is likely to emerge. Sexual attractors are complex. Their origins and appeals at times seem incomprehensible despite what may seem to be an irresistible seduction. It may seem that they "just are," because no other explanation appears.

Then there are the many models of possible identification, and attendant objects of attraction, that are presented to everyone, and that have varying degrees of personal appeal. For example, in a particular case the idea of being gay may appear to offer the greatest narcissistic satisfaction, but this is not a universal explanation for being gay. Explanations for the origination of sexual preferences or orientations have to be customized.

The multiplicity of motivations for choosing the way a person demonstrates personal gender identity shifts the focus away from developmental markers, such as psychosexual or psychosocial stages, to patterns or mosaics of development. Biological factors will influence the time of certain sexual activities, such as puberty and the dominance of genital sensations for sexual excitation, but the normative concept of sexual preference is clearly marked as a social construction. The mainstream is already becoming wider in terms of viable sexual preferences. For example, in some way, living a gay or lesbian life style has become easier and more acceptable, although still ground for social criticism. It is quite likely that the glorification of heterosexuality, and the social pressure to conform to that norm, will decrease with the acceptance of the idea that living a different life is not pathological. The pathology of sex lies in what a person does with his/her sexuality, intentions, the meanings attached to his/her interests and actions, but not in whether one has a same sex or opposite-sex partner, or is bisexual, or has no partner, or no children. This issue was amply discussed by Freud (1905) in his concept of perversion where he puts the nature of pathology not in the act itself but in the meaning, in the associated fantasy.

The question still remains as to how one develops a sexual life style. The process of development indicates that much of it is learned by imitating others, as well as through interaction. In addition to an instinctual component, a certain amount is contributed by physical maturation of skills and brain mechanisms. Added to this is the uniqueness of each person, so that skills such as walking, talking, and style, are "as if' skills, similar to what other people do, but not identical. All of this is contained within a broad conception of identification, or internalized through the developmental steps of introjection, identification, and identity formation, and includes subjective and intersubjective socialization. The result is a psychobiological process that has certain approximate phases, but is not universally deterministic, e.g., everybody does not talk.

The exceptions to the most customary developmental patterns can be investigated for etiology, both physical and psychological. Sometimes the etiology appears to involve an interaction of psychic and somatic factors, and sometimes the etiology remains a mystery, e.g., autism.

When it comes to sexuality, the expected pattern of development appears to proceed from relatively undifferentiated objects of preference and bodily excitations to gendered preferences and a genital focus. Different specifics of excitation appear along gendered lines, but the capacity for orgasm appears open to all, regardless of gender. These specifics are influenced by biological forces and by social forces, with the socialmoral superego, along with the ego, dictating what are appropriate sexual expressions. Thus far, the heterosexual model prevails, but this seems more of a social construction than an instinctual response. As a result, sexuality is potentially fluid in all its psychic aspects.

As some sexual patterns have become more open in some situations and socially accepted, particularly same-sex choices and bisexuality, the pathology of the unusual has come into question. This has led, for example, to depathologizing homosexuality, but in the process, has often resulted in assuming a biological essentialism that has been used in the past to undergird the naturalness of heterosexuality.

For example, a male patient states, "I have always been attracted to men."

"Can you recall when you first noticed this?"

"Oh, more or less. I mean, I was young, and I got the picture that I was supposed to like girls, that boys naturally did. I mean, I liked girls, but not that way."

"They did not excite you sexually?"

"Not really, not like boys."

"Why do you think you felt that way?"

"I have no idea, really. I mean, if you are thinking it was how my parents raised me, or Uncle Teddy gave me head when I was six, not the case. My father was a jock, my brothers are jocks, in fact, hell, my sisters are all athletes."

"Meaning?"

"Well I'm not. I wasn't, ever."

"Liking an athlete, being an athlete, that doesn't determine your sexual orientation."

"Yes, well, you know, there is this idea that gays are feminine, and that women are not that into sports."

"Is that it, you believe you are feminine?"

"No, no, I don't. In fact, I think, to be honest, that real men prefer sex with other men, that it is more masculine."

The analyst is silent, as is the patient. Then the patient says, "Look, no offense to you, I mean I know you're married, but I don't know your sexual history, or what you would really like to do."

The analyst laughs. "Maybe I don't either, but let's figure we can each be real men without having to like or do the same things."

"You don't want to tell me what you really like to do, sexually?"

"Whatever moves me, provided it doesn't harm me or anybody else, is what comes to mind. Why does it matter?"

"I want to be sure you understand me, how I feel, who I am sexually."

"I'm not you, but surely that doesn't prevent me from understanding you, anymore than you not being me has to hinder your understanding of me."

"True enough. You've obviously dealt with these kinds of objections before." "Sounding me out seems sensible. Now let me sound you out some more. You feel you have always been gay?"

"Yes. It was there. I was born gay, I suppose. Anyway, does it really matter given that I like being gay and have no interest in changing?"

"Analysts like complete pictures. It helps me understand you." "Implying it would help me understand myself?"

"Yes, it could. The whole process, our relationship, is about possibilities."

"So maybe you think I had a choice, gay or straight, or whatever?"

"We both are aware that I can only know what you tell me, which is that you feel you were always gay. That doesn't sound as if you feel you made a choice, or had one to make."

"But you're picking up that I'm defensive about being gay?"

"I get that little tinge of guilt, as though even being gay without having any choice isn't really all right, that you believe there is something wrong with you." "Because I am gay?"

"That could be one reason. Homophobia is all over the place, being out can be risky, but I would guess that is only part of it. The way I tend to think about you is that you are unhappy with the person you are. My focus is person, before man, before gay."

'You're sure you are not gay?"

They both laugh.

This is a typical segment in our experience with gay and lesbian patients. They often do not feel certain of the origins of their sexual preference, but can describe their beginning awareness of their sexual preference. Straight patients tend to be the same, but aren't questioned about this so often. The idea of having no choice is appealing because it relieves the guilt engendered by society. However, each orientation wants to embrace this position in a different personalized pattern. For example, straight people believe it is natural to be that way, and that being gay in not natural. This is accompanied by the conclusion that homosexuality is chosen, because it isn't natural. Gay and lesbian people view origins as consisting of a number of natural positions which in turn are not freely chosen, but given to each person. Of course, this is a big issue because homosexuality was considered pathology, and because many heterosexuals see other orientations as a threat to family structure. Also, to avoid social criticism, many marginalized groups, as pedophiles, would like to claim their approach was natural, but most of the mainstream, including homosexuals, would be reluctant to include these other groups without considering many of them as disturbed people. In addition to the issue of logical inconsistency, we have previously noted that there is not convincing evidence for biological determinism for any orientation. This is not, however, equivalent to feeling that one has a choice, or that a choice could bring satisfaction. While there are many possibilities, the most appealing course feels set, even though there may also be conflict about pursuing it. Could a person be different? That often appears possible, but not effectively desirable. As Bartelby the Scribener said long ago in the Melville story, "I prefer not to."

In discussing the potential flexibility of sexuality, the point has been made that in considering "situational sexuality," as in prison, "Rather than focusing on the limitation of choice, ... consider instead the individual's *willingness* to choose in *spite* of limited options" (Parker & DeCecco, 1995, p.429).

Our emphasis is on preference within multiplicity, thereby avoiding the so-called naturalness that is ultimately reductionistic to a limited number of forms of sexuality. At the same time, there is acceptance of the idea that it may well feel "natural" to have a specific sexual orientation.

In the case material for this patient to follow, the presenting problem was depression. He felt this was due to the dissolution of a relationship where he had been rejected. The fact that he was gay was discussed in analysis within the context of understanding both his identity and his relationships. More of the details of his sexual behavior would need to be discussed in order to have a better comprehension of his sexuality. The self categorization as gay, straight, bisexual, implies certain sexual behaviors, but other behaviors, as sadomasochism, are not linked to a category. So, in discussing sexual preference, consideration needs to be given to both the choice of partners and sexual activities with these partners, and with the self.

For example, a male patient reports dissatisfaction with his sexual life. "My wife doesn't really like to do it that much."

"I am not sure what you mean. Is it that she isn't interested enough in sex, or that she isn't interested often enough?"

"Both, really, but I'm thinking about how little we do it."

"How little she is willing to have sexual intercourse with you?"

"Yes. Actually any kind of physical contact. She thinks affection will lead to me wanting to have sex with her."

"Will it?"

"I suppose that's often on my mind."

"What is on your mind when you do have sex with her?" "You mean, what do I think about?"

"Yes, what do you think about during sex with your wife?"

He laughs ironically. "Better get this over with fast or she'll be pissed." "Anything else? You know, do you have a fantasy?"

The patient appears embarrassed. He shifts his bodily position before speaking again. "I like to think about spanking her ass."

"I suppose that could be because you are angry at her, but could it also be that the idea turns you on?"

"It isn't because I am angry."

"You thought about the spanking before?"

"It is what I think about when I have sex."

"When you masturbate?"

"Yes."

"Have you ever spanked a woman as part of having sex?"

"No. no. I've never even told any woman I would want to." "But you do want to?"

"Yes. I'm probably perverted."

"That's what you think all women would say about you if they knew what you wanted?"

"Sure."

"From what you are telling me about your wife, I can see your reluctance to tell her, but, all women?"

"Look, I told you even though you are a woman because I am desperate, because I need help, because maybe somehow my wife knows and it turns her off. But you think it's perverted. I know it."

"At the risk of implying anything about my sex life, which I do not wish to do, I don't think what you told me is something for you to feel guilty about. Sex is often about dominance and submission, which can be shown in a lot of ways, spanking included. Also, particularly important in your situation, is that it is what you are thinking about, not doing, or telling. It is yours alone."

Here the man began by stating a preference for more frequent sexual intercourse, then provided additional material about sado-masochistic thoughts and desires, as well as indicating his guilt. His sex role identity is multi-layered, which is often the situation, and sex is associated with guilt because he is thinking outside what he believes is the norm, which is another issue that is frequently encountered. This segment highlights the probability that sexuality as a social construction will put a positive spin on "doing it the right way." However, even when a norm has been developed, or a patient judges personal behavior in such terms, the "right way," is not the only way to express healthy sexuality. As the analyst in this case noted, there are numerous "right ways."

By opening up the developmental possibilities, there is less of a direct tie to markers, such as stages, but this can still be a useful approach in beginning exploration. The initial hope of psychoanalysis was a clear correspondence with fixations at psychosexual stages to specific psychopathology. That hope has faded, and the same limited expectations apply to tying specific relational or self- growth experiences to symptom patterns. At the same time, some connections can be made. These are more hints than certainties, but these hints are useful. In the case of sexuality, the search is for personal attractors that at least may correlate with sexual expression, and at times, may offer significant explanations. Sexual preferences are based on these attractors, these personal definitions of masculinity, femininity, or crossing lines. They represent special meanings that are connected to the internalization process, with the identifications based on personal needs rather than gender rules. The next chapter explores the many patterns of desire that result from these personal attractors.

Chapter 4

CREATIVE EXPRESSIONS

DEVELOPMENTAL PATHWAYS

There are a large number of developmental lines that lead to what can be considered healthy sexuality. This view differs from the classical position that there is one healthy resolution to the Oedipal position and that is heterosexuality. Other sexual preferences are defensive and pathological. It also differs from the relational position that sexuality is one way of demonstrating a connection to others, but attachment is the primary motivation in sexual expression. Instead, we view sexuality as integrating drives and relations so that it is psychobiological with fluid and diverse manifestations. In both quantitative and qualitative terms, sexuality will vary across people and within the individual, but it is always a basic component of personal identity. That is, we are looking for a widening of the scope of inquiry with regard to sexual desire in ways that have not been possible with the current psychoanalytic conceptualizations.

A significant forerunner to our reconstruction of sexuality appears in the work of Harding (2001). She has brought together a series of essays by a number of authors, all of whom build on the idea that sex originates as polymorphous and develops through the influence of both psychological and biological forces. As a result, there is a significant expansion of the bandwidth for healthy sexuality.

This is akin to our belief in a fundamental instinctual bisexuality, which is subsequently converted into a more specific sexual preference. This conversion process takes place for adaptive purposes, namely that each person sees a particular sexuality as most conducive to their overall well being. A key feature in the process is identification, which includes both the ability to imitate the other as well as to fantasize being the other, and can operate at unconscious and conscious levels.

Mitzler (1979) had described a metapsychology for homosexual object choice that followed the basic guidelines of Oedipal resolution, but reinterpreted the process. Mendoza (2001) notes that, in this model, bisexuality is the ability to identify with both parents rather than having sexual relations with either of them. The latter becomes possible because of the identifications, boy as girl, girl as boy, so that in fantasy there is still heterosexuality. However, that type of metapsychology is inaccurate because it requires that gay men think of themselves as women and lesbians think of themselves as men. This can happen, but our experience indicates that gender identity is usually intact in homosexuality, but object choice shifts from opposite sex to same sex. Thus a focus on imagined identification, to the relative exclusion of preference, marginalizes homosexuality.

Instead, the identification process results in a man who prefers men, and a woman who prefers women, as sexual partners. This does away with the idea that being masculine or feminine necessarily includes the choice of a different-gendered partner. The instinctive bisexuality means options in personally defining gender characteristics. Gender is both empowered and bound by biology. Within this context, it is what one makes of it, and that provides many healthy possibilities, along with pathological ones. Also, in the process of fashioning a personal sexuality, it is necessary to cope with the most frequent social models that exist at the time. Thus, traditional masculinity and femininity will operate as barriers for anyone who wants to be, or is, different. However, these are only obstacles, not immutable rules of psychic health or illness.

The process of identification has been misused to foster the cultural rigidity of being male or female. Internalization, which involves the formation of both self-representations and object-representations, has been equated with stereotyped gender roles that demand an equation between gender and heterosexual activity. This then becomes a sanitized version of internalization, which keeps intact the customary family structure that results from the traditional version of the Oedipal resolution and the reproductive process in evolution. This is one possible course, but not the only one that is healthy and adaptive.

Relational approaches are not an improvement in building from an Oedipal platform in regard to sexual options. Even if one pays limited attention to developmental stages, parent-child relationships become attachment templates that for sexuality tend to point in a conventional direction. For example, the value of sexual excitement is considered quite limited unless it is aimed at forming relationships (Harding, 2001). The idea of sexual excitement for personal satisfaction only, is viewed as pathologically narcissistic.

Also problematic is a proposed reinterpretation of projective identification. This has customarily been looked upon as a process in which a disturbing part of the self is projected into another and then the person projecting can safely identify with this part, as aggression, because it is still owned by the self but contained by another. Identification is used to maintain the connection, to retain a sense of intactness, but projection is used to keep a safe distance from the disturbance. The process is defensive, designed to protect the self through the use of an external object. Mendoza (2001) splits the concept into an intrusive process, which is negative, and a communicative process, which is positive. The latter is essentially a type of intersubjectivity in which the feelings of another are felt as one's own at the same time as they are experienced as belonging to the other person. This interpretation does not fit with our experience. We have found the patient experiencing relief through the use of projective identification because of the containment by the analyst. However, the analyst as the container experiences discomfort with the feelings of the other as they pervade the feelings of the analyst. Thus, from the container's point of view the process is both communicative and intrusive, and it depends on the analyst's ability to contain as to whether the patient's efforts bring any sustained relief or fail.

Projective identification is a concept that is open to reinterpretation, however, so we will mention another possibility. Each part of the process could be considered as elements of introjection in the mode of identification. Thus, projection could be viewed as the capacity to understand a personal feeling as normative. For example, projecting one's anger into someone else is designed to provide a justification for one's own anger, but it also makes it clear to the projecting person that others get angry. In this vein, anger, or any projected affect, is a shared, communal emotion that calls for a response. This is a learning process in that the projection is not necessarily correct just because it is made, but remains of value even if it is mistaken in a specific instance, because it allows experimentation with the range of possible affects available to people.

When the projection is coupled with identification, the result provides an understanding of what it would be like if the projecting person was the other, at least in regard to that particular affect. The process expedites interesubjective movement such as seeing the other as a subject, a self, as well as an object, because to some degree the self and the other become one. However, it is not the same as understanding the subjectivity of the other as distinct from the self of the projecting person, because the subjectivity belongs to the projector. Someone else is you, and you are someone else, by your creation, not due to an understanding of the feelings of another that arise from within that person as contrasted with being projected there.

The revisionist attempts at providing an appropriate explanation for sexuality have primarily been redefinitions of terms and concepts that have some utility in providing possibilities for clarification, but fall short of the extensive elaboration already given by the existing combination of psychosexual and psychosocial stages. However, these have the original problematic aspects that have led to trying to make the changes that have been suggested, so certain refinements are needed.

Attempts at splitting terms, such as polymorphous from perverse, or genital from phallic, keep the either/or approach dividing healthy from pathological rather than explaining the multiplicity of sexual options. Also, these can be questionable distinctions, particularly when the ultimate result is the same as if one used the original term. For example, polymorphous perverse was intended to illustrate more than polarity, given the infantile diffusion of cause, aim, and object that was represented by the concept. As psychosexual development proceeded, there was a reduction in both the polymorphous and the perverse aspects of sexuality. The polymorphous conception was itself perverse. Mendoza (2001) actually describes polymorphous impulses as being infantile and regressive, although in service of the ego. He gives them a positive spin without disputing their origin. However, to make polymorphous into bisexuality, and in turn to make multiplicity viable, it would be necessary to alter the original intent of the concept, which appears to be the description of a transitional process. Our experience indicates that diversity of cause, aim, and purpose has the potential to be available throughout the life cycle for healthy as well as pathological expression. Thus, transitional can be reinterpreted. Instead of meaning that the concept has to be designed to be socialized away in favor of a focused heterosexuality, it can mean it is available to be used in different ways at different times. As such, a metapsychology, whether instinctual or relational, exists as an explanation of sexual development.

Another problematic example is a proposed additional distinction between phallic and genital. Mendoza sees phallic sexuality as drive satisfaction without concern for the object, whereas genital sexuality involves object relations, which makes genital better than phallic. First of all, such a distinction is likely to lead to more confusion because of the many other ways phallic is already used in psychoanalysis. One example is the phallic stage, which precedes the genital stage where both stages are part of drive theory. Then there is Jung's use of the phallus as a powerful tool with potentials to be both destructive and creative, and finally there is Lacan's emphasis on the phallus as a lack, which fosters desire for men as an ideal, and for women as an object to be possessed.

A second problem is the repeated glorification of relational sex as opposed to personal sexual excitement. We have already mentioned this approach in the work of Harding (2001). Mendoza has a similar view, stating, "The aspect of love which is excitement must therefore be the containment of phallic drive within genital regard" (2001, p.162).

The issue seems to be a need to demarcate healthy from pathological sex, which in turn is related to Freud's original concern about the relationship between pathology and appropriate sexual expression. These are certainly legitimate concerns, but the need for explanation seems to be causing a rush to judgment that becomes moralizing about sexuality. For example, even though homosexuality is gaining acceptance as not necessarily pathological, the idea of good and bad sex persists in a normative moral fashion. Such an approach continues to marginalize homosexuality, despite the fact that this is sexual activity with another person.

A complicated schema exists containing levels of approved sexuality. In addition to heterosexuality getting the highest approval, relational sexuality is considered the apex of heterosexuality, and within relational sex, intersubjective sex gets the highest grade for its focus on consideration of the totality of the object of desire. Such grading pushes sexuality away from an emphasis on instinctual pleasure and toward object relations as a goal. However, as we have noted throughout, divorcing sexuality from instinct runs counter to patients' reports of their sexual experiences. Although it is possible that patient descriptions are social constructions at least some of the time, this does not rule out the possibility that some of the time they are not. Also, the social construction can be defensive, so it is possible to doubt either a relational or an instinctual emphasis reported by a patient. Our impression is that despite the current emphasis on relating, attachment, and connection, all of which would tend to reinforce patient descriptions of sexuality in those terms, instinctual depictions have a frequency that support their validity.

In this context, Mendoza states, "The rapprochement of object related and drive directed metapsychologies give us the flexibility that patients need us to have" (2001, p.163).

Maintaining the connection between the instinctual and the relational runs parallel to a tie between the intrapsychic and the interpersonal. These are connections that appear experientially validated, but why make one type of sexuality better than the other? It appears to be a social phenomenon where the support of personal sexual gratification is quite limited (Stein, 1998), but the support for sex with objects is plentiful (Green, 1997; Harding, 2001). This is akin to saying superego sex is the good stuff, but id sex is bad for you, unless transformations occur to move the id in a more acceptable direction, namely the direction of the object and the intersubjective.

Why not accept the possibility that narcissistic sex is different from object-related sex without making one type better than the other? We return to our previous question, with the acceptance that behavior is judged by society. However, the rightness or wrongness of sexuality needs to be seen as contextual and contingent. It does not automatically depend on the presence or absence of objects, or on consideration, attachment, or connection. Better distinctions are drawn between motivations for sex that illustrate the different possibilities, and the different pathways leading to these motivations.

Here are some clinical examples.

"I enjoy masturbation because I feel as if I have complete control over my orgasms."

"I just wanted to get laid."

"I have never felt so connected in my life."

Different motivations, different satisfactions, all possible as part of sexuality. None have to be considered superior, anymore than sexuality has to be considered instinctual or relational primarily, or gender has to be either genetic or socially constructed. Contextuality, which Stolorow (1997) has aptly depicted, or contingency, most recently described by Dimen (2004), are more experiential and closer to the truth, uncomfortable to many as it may continue to be. The acceptance of healthy narcissism (Herron, 1999), as well as pathological, is congruent with these conceptions. There is a strong need to get past the good-bad framework in regard to understanding sexuality. Any person's sexual interests or behavior may make people uncomfortable, but that is not an automatic sign of the pathological nature of the sexuality.

At the moment, the pathways to sexual expression tend to focus on shifts in the process, as, for example, the results of fantasies of exclusion from the parental relationship, or modifications in the psychosexual or psychosocial concepts already proposed. For example, using early genital as a more accurate term for both genders than the phallic stage, or emphasizing evidence supporting relationality from birth instead of infantile autism.These approaches are useful, but limited. The first applies to attempts to understand development where the result has been considered clearly pathological. Unfortunately, although in regard to sexuality shifts have taken place in opinions regarding the pathology, developmental explanations connected to a pathological outcome have often remained. Homosexuality is an example of this. The orientation has been depathologized without providing an accompanying normalized developmental process. Of course, it is possible that reactions to developmental events affect sexuality, but these reactions are not necessarily the causes of heterosexuality or homosexuality. Instead, they are more likely to be contributors to the motivations and styles of being straight or gay or bisexual.

In regard to the second area of exploration, changes in aspects of the developmental lines, certainly a lot has been gained in terms of understanding self development, relational interactions, and the repositioning of female sexuality. At the moment, however, there is more of an acceptance of different possibilities for sexuality than there are explanations of their origins.

Also, a distinction needs to be made between the dynamics of a sexual orientation and the dynamics of sexual behavior. They are interconnected, but have points of separation. For example, a preference for sadomasochistic sexuality is not limited to gender preference for partners, nor is child molestation, or other controversial sexual behaviors. At the same time, gender choice can limit the choice of a sexual activity. For example, a partner's lack of a penis or a vagina. Also, despite the range of possibilities available, some people will have a preference that is not a function of the gender of the partners, as oral sex. Considering these mixtures, it is necessary to try to understand the reasons for choice of behaviors, partners, and orientations. Choice is used here to refer to the exercise of sexual possibilities. At the same time, it is understood that in specific instances people may not feel as if they have options.

PARTNER CHOICE

In most instances there is a primary caretaker for a child. There could be such a division of care taking that would equalize caretakers, but it is unlikely as a care taking arrangement, and, even if it were set up that way, a child is unlikely to have that view of the process. Also, even when the person doing most of the care is not the biological mother or father, the identity of the actual mother and father are usually made clear to the child. In addition, although there are instances where others appear to do more direct parenting, the "mothering" functions are generally depicted to the child as the property of the mother. Functions customarily performed by fathers, even if performed by mothers or others, have a similar crossover fate, namely they are considered "fathering," and, as such, belonging to the father. With some exceptions, the customary result is that regardless of single-sex parenting, or same-sex parents, or parenting by proxy, the child is made aware of the traditional functional relationships. Even if it is fantasy, children are socialized to accept this view in most instances. Children learn what mothers are expected to do for them, and what fathers are expected to do for them, as well as how they are supposed to feel about their actual parents. This learning is generally effective, regardless of who carries out the parental functions and who would appear to deserve the child's love. Despite considerable conflict, a wished-for family system often turns reality into a traditional fantasy.

Connected to this social process is the awareness of being gendered. This means doing masculine or feminine things, socially defined, in accord with the child's gender. A recognition of anatomical gendered characteristics also takes place, along with the creation of self and object representations, and differentiation of self and others, as well as other cognitive and affective developments.

All of this makes up the broad process of internalization whereby an inner world is created for both internal and external stimuli. There is a recognition of sexual feelings and pleasure, as well as an interest in having these occur. This sexuality appears to be instinctually derived and then expressed with the self and others. Internalization involves the development of sexual preferences that are partially based on gender role identities, and partially based on cross-identifications, or "gender bending."

Certainly, a significant amount of sexual identity is a social construction that influences sexual preference, such as the heterosexual option for both genders. Because of an original diversity of interest regarding partners, as well as self-stimulation without the need for partners, sexual orientation appears to originate as options. This is not an either-or situation, but a multiplicity of possibilities, any or all of which can appear desirable, and be explored. However, due to powerful social norms, there is pressure on the individual that accompanies heightened genital interest. The result frequently is that sexual orientation feels as though it was predetermined so that there are no options, nor did they ever exist. In most societies the expected orientation is heterosexual, but if the actual desired orientation is something other than heterosexual, that may feel as though it was predetermined. In situations other than heterosexuality, a different type of social construction prevails. Personal attractors cause a person to feel that sexual needs will be best met by a particular orientation, but that orientation has been marginalized. The person can feel justified in seeking social approval provided that the orientation is just as natural as heterosexuality is for another person.

The belief in biological determinism for the origins of sexual orientation appears to be largely an unconscious process, although there are instances where people report conflict about expressing a preference. This conflict is different from conflict resulting from having a marginalized sexual orientation. In the former case, the conflict is between possibilities, as for example heterosexuality or homosexuality. In the latter, conflict is the result of an orientation, such as negative social reaction to being gay or lesbian. Our focus at this point is on origins. The etiology appears to be an inherent pansexualism, which derives specifics, such as orientation, from experience. Sensual pleasure is one example. Safety is another possibility. The fantasy of an erotic connection with opposite-sex partners, for example, may seem dangerous based on accumulated fantasies and experiences. A similar situation may exist for bisexuality where the involvement with only one gender could appear restrictive and dangerous. Heterosexuality has the greatest social support and the least possibility of being marginalized, in turn, fostering its appeal. There are numerous reasons for the appeal of a sexual orientation, but these origins are usually repressed, and often remain unconscious, with a set of conscious beliefs becoming dominant, although they may not correspond to the actual origins.

We have made a point of the need for recognizing the patient's experience. In the light of questioning essentialism, we are not expressing doubt about the fact that this is the patient's belief, but we are aware that this is an implication that the patient is drawing based on feelings at that time. The origins have been repressed and often remain inaccessible, so essentially they are unknown. Based on the polymorphous character of sexuality, and the available research that we cited previously, orientation is open rather than predetermined. This means that sexuality is potentially fluid with the possibility of gender role choices, but for most people it often does not feel that way. Instead, it feels set, natural, and satisfying, as long as the sexual orientation that is being followed is the one that is primarily desired. When desire conflicts with convention, or with an orientation that one is attempting to follow, then applying determinism to desire provides a socially acceptable way out of the conflict, as well as satisfying desire. Adding to the appeal of determinism being applied to a desired orientation is that unfortunately people with interests other than heterosexual have too often felt social pressure to somehow change their desires, or at least act that way. Such an approach does not solve the conflict and is unsatisfactory, but it is not necessary to force essentialism upon an orientation in order to justify it. Polymorphous sexuality provides everyone with the opportunity to express their sexual feelings in a variety of ways. Some barriers to doing that are a function of adaptations required by the development of civilization, but others avoid the potential of the instinctive multiplicity of desire due to fear and ignorance about consequences. The exclusive equation of heterosexuality with healthy sex is the most potent example, because it is not healthy for everybody. At the same time, certain forms of sexual expression can be detrimental, and therefore are not acceptable. For instance, heterosexual expression of desire may be fraught with a great deal of malevolent transformations and perversion of aim and object, etc. as well. The result is that healthy sexuality does involve selective expression that is adaptive, but not as restrictive as the social norms of the past would suggest.

The concept of options involves mixed potentials. It increases the range of natural sexual expression, which in turn reduces the sexual behaviors that have been considered pathological. Such a conclusion needs to be based on the motivations for the behavior and the results of the behavior, as opposed to negation by category. Also, multiplicity provides a way to understand shifts in sexuality. These can occur because they are available.

The other aspect of the issue is that the concept of option has also been used paradoxically to be restrictive. Options have been equated with conscious choices, and incorporated into a view that sees everyone as able to choose heterosexuality. Accompanying this is pressure for everyone to make that choice, as well as negativity regarding people who make a different choice. However, having options is not the same as feeling a person has these options, and people usually do not report_feeling as though options were available. Sexual orientation, and sexual behavior, often have a compulsive quality that goes unnoticed by many people because they are comfortable enough with what is happening. The questioning comes from those who experience conflict, and even then the conflict has to be significant. Sexuality involves an erotic imagination that is quite encompassing, shame and guilt accompanying pleasure and satisfaction. Basically, it is common for there to be a mixture of good and bad, comfort and discomfort, that is accepted in a dissociative process that allows a positive view of the sexual experience to dominate. However, because of that mixture, constructed by experience over time, the possibility of conflict is there. The probability of its emergence is greatest when the sexual activities have already developed the stain of social or moral stigma.

The negative possibilities that are derived from options, and the accompanying diversity of sexual fantasies, can be avoided by understanding that sexuality is most satisfying and acceptable to the individual when it is a personal construction that acknowledges cultural and biological influences, but is not ruled by inner or outer demons. Personal sexual identity is open, although it often may feel determined as each person discovers what is satisfying at the time, and in turn, views that as destiny. Some people reevaluate this destiny, while others stay with the idea. There is no single ideal in this regard, but there remains the possibilities of multiplicity, diversity, and alternatives that could be more satisfying. Staying in touch with the twists and turns of desire can be both threatening and enhancing.

Blocking sexual satisfaction can be detrimental to one's health, depending on the circumstances, as Freud so forcefully noted. Finding the most adaptive approach to that satisfaction is, at the same time, quite a task. Sexuality scares people as well as comforts them, so there is ambivalence, and in turn, resistance to opening up sexual boundaries. Despite that, there has been expansion, reinforcing the need to understand and facilitate this growth. The aim is to have more appropriate boundaries, which does involve some containment. Good sexuality is akin to freedom in that it works within limits. Given that qualification, the limits for sexuality have been anxiety-driven too often. This has caused suffering for people who have been marginalized based on norms that were socially constructed in a defensive manner. The harm in such construction is notable because sexual differences are pathologized as sexual offenses with serious consequences for the people involved. With that in mind, our next step is to take a closer look at existing sexual norms.

The Heterosexual Norm

Sexual role identity is part of the overall process of internalization. The process is also often described as identification, although that is just one of the steps included in internalization. The complete process eventuates in creating a self through experiences with others as well as the active development of fantasy. The sexual self that is created represents preferences for sexual activities and sexual partners. An example of the former is a proposal by Davies (Levine, 2004) of two sexual self-systems, good and bad object sexuality. Each system has its own affects, ideas, and body experiences, e.g.,good sex embodies romantic love, with bad sex emphasizing stimulation, and they coexist to contain each other. Such a conception illustrates the influence of social expectations, which are especially prominent when considering sexual preference. The most frequent expectation is for opposite-sex partners, as well as a preference for both genders to get married and have children. Same-sex marriage, a hot topic in the most recent United States presidential election, and a possibility that appeared to disturb the majority of the population of that country, would not be considered acceptable. The perpetuation of the traditional family structure is generally consistent with the norms of most societies, although there are variations in the traditional mother-father role structure based on ethnic and marital status distinctions. For example, there has been a significant increase in the number of single-parent families, families where both parents work, and in the number of children in day care. These results mean alterations in family structure that affect the possibilities for identification.

Identification with the same-sex parent, when there is one available as a model, has been viewed as incorporating the gender preference of that parent, but not necessarily the specifics of the parent's sexual behavior, such as position, activity, or fantasy. The specifics of sexual activity are usually discovered from a variety of sources, with the parents supplying only the basics, if that. As a result, that identification is primarily an extra-familial social construction, namely "this is what men do, this is what women do," in contrast to "this is what I do," as a description by either mother or father.

Erotic interest in another person is more likely to be based on direct contact with caretakers. Based on frequency of contact with children, mothers or females who would appear to serve as mother-figures, have long been viewed as the first object of desire. The idea has high probability, but could occur at such an early age that it is difficult to verify. So, it is possible that a gay man who feels he was born gay did have an erotic attachment to his mother that shifted in terms of subsequent gender preference, but it remains repressed, or he may not. The type of attachment would seem very dependent on the quality of the mothering, specifically how erotic it is, based both on the mother's actions and the child's reactions. It is also possible that a male caretaker, or a fantasized male, could supersede the mother or female caretaker in this area. Another possibility is that an original attachment to the mother needs to be preserved by a male. This is then accomplished by subsequently having sex only with men, so the mother is never replaced by another woman. Also open for consideration is the degree to which identification and desire are merged, because sexual union can represent being the other person.

The variations on identification and erotic attachment also apply to women. If a girl models herself closely on her mother, she will follow her mother's gender preference for a sexual partner. If she has a stronger identification with a different model, that is what she will pursue. There are a very large number of possibilities for both genders. Within these possibilities there are expected and usual attractors for erotic attachment, such as pleasurable physical contact, but there are also unexpected and unusual attractors, and fantasy life plays a large role in promoting attachments and excitement. The result is the lack of a clear picture and the inability to make definitive predictions, or to conceptualize a developmental theory that does not have a significant number of exceptions to any concise explanation.

However, assuming the parents provide "good-enough loving," a child is likely to imitate some of their characteristics and direct varying degrees of sexual desire toward each of them. The concept of erotic denotes a special type of appeal and pleasure, primarily sensory and instinctive. The feeling of love for another does not always have an erotic component. However, when the love is erotic it is not always given to the best caretaker. There is probably strong unconscious motivation involved, causing confusion as to the reason for the desire, which often includes erotic feelings toward "bad" objects, as well as others that are not loved, but sexually desired. Joining love and sexual feelings was presented by Freud as an ideal considered to be genital love. This view is also very much a part of relational and self theories, but sexuality does not begin this way. Also, as it develops there is not a complete shift to the world of objects outside of the self. A strong narcissistic component remains.

However, the world of objects certainly fills up a great deal of space devoted to the satisfaction of desire. The way others treat the developing child, as well as the child's reactions and fantasies about others, coalesce with biological processes to foster sexual interest in others. It does appear likely that early attachments have erotic components, thus supporting the idea that in addition to the self there is an initial external object for sexual feelings. This person usually appears to be the mother, or the mothering person, who, by proximity, provides the sensory contact and stimulation likely to arouse sexual interest. However, the degree to which that interest is perceived by the person as gendered, and in particular, reflecting interest in a female, is unknown. At the same time, there is a social learning process that fosters gender-specific masculine and feminine positions. These usually include opposite-sex partners for both genders, and always mean erotic love for both parents needs to be subordinated in both feelings and expression. Sexual desire is destined to be moved outside of the family as well as beyond the self. This requires identity modification. Given the probability of the mother being the first object for whom both genders are likely to have erotic feelings, as well as the first object to be incorporated, the changes required are complex for both boys and girls. At this point in our discussion we will assume that the mother is perceived by the children as feminine and the father as masculine.

Based on the existence of sexual desire, the boy has a choice of sexual objects, but the anatomical differences between the boy and his mother prevent physical identification based on body similarity. He is also restricted by social pressure from identifying with the mother's object choice. In contrast, the girl can identify bodily and socially with her mother. For both genders these identifications have a primary level, with the same-sex parent, and a secondary level, with the opposite-sex parent. Despite the polymorphous nature of sexuality, a more restrictive path is usually taken. That path is in accord with the primary level of identification, although both genders suffer some loss, namely the replacement of their original connections between attachment and erotic interest in their parents. They are forced to differentiate these feelings. Also, to the degree that the parents varied as models of femininity and masculinity, a child will make comparisons with other models that may be encountered, so identification will be selective.

The losses that occur are buffered by the process of adaptation. Although the mother usually is the first object for both genders, the father is also the object of attachment and affection. As a result, each parent complements the other and mitigates the loss of the other to some degree. There is also a realistic barrier to the child's level of possession of either parent, and that is that the parents are attached to each other. In addition, sublimation of love for the parents has its own appeal. These buffers help the child in subsequently seeking erotic objects who are age-appropriate, regardless of their gender.

Following a particular gender role does mean accepting some degree of loss throughout a person's sexual life, because some possibilities need to be given up in favor of other possibilities. Gender roles are usually not thought of in this way, but the process of giving up what is desired that has been noted in regard to each parent, is a process that is repeated in various ways in the development of other relational patterns. However, the loss is adaptively turned into the value derived from selection, even when the selection feels preordained, or is partially that way, e.g., anatomical differences.

It seems likely that in attempting to explain the reasons for any sexual orientation, some of the attractors will remain unknown. They are formed from combinations of instinct, experience, the personal appeal of a variety of sources, and social constructions, that are not sufficiently accessible to conscious knowledge. These are factored in with what can be known. The path that is followed, ultimately, is what seems to be most compelling personally. At this time in our history, heterosexuality wins the prize, but is no guarantee of satisfaction or freedom from conflict. Nor is any orientation, given the diverse nature of sexuality as relatively solitary force. Of course, it is not solitary, but embedded within a personality where adaptation eventually dominates. Adaptation requires loss, mistakes, and limits on self-expression as each person seeks their own version of an ego-ideal. Whatever sexuality predominates, some compromise will be included.

Gay, Lesbian, and Bisexual Patterns

Developmental pathways for sexuality that result in orientations other than the heterosexual norm involve different identifications based on different attractors. These could be fostered directly by the primary caretakers, but that does not usually seem to occur. Our evidence for this is that patients have never told us that this was the case, and gay parents often make the point that they do not influence any children they have to follow in their footsteps. This is in contrast to heterosexual couples and appears to be a political issue. If gay parents were to follow the pattern of straight parents in attempting to influence sexual orientation to match their own, they could reduce their opportunities to be accepted as parents by society. Such a result is likely to offset parental attitudes that favor being gay over being straight. Of course, unconscious attempts at orientation- persuasion may still occur. Also, there have been indirect examples, such as "feminizing" the male, or doing the opposite to the female, but correlation between these approaches and choice of a partner's gender are low. Creating a family atmosphere that is directly aimed at firmly establishing a particular sexual orientation, usually heterosexual, is no guarantee that it will happen. While others can seemingly make one choice look more attractive than another for some time, that is ultimately not the decisive factor. There has to be a connection between internal determinants and external possibilities. Experience can contribute to predispositions as well as providing opportunities, but there have to be personal attractors. As noted, their origins can be particularly obscure. Whatever type of sexuality that is central to an adaptive ego structure may be defensive, or it may be congruent with positive feelings about the self and others. Such possibilities apply to all sexual orientations.

In a defensive situation the choice of a sexual orientation rests upon perceived advantages that include strong unconscious influences. For example, a married woman separated from her husband, with whom she had an unsatisfactory relationship. She then became involved with a woman, and was living with her when she began treatment. Their sexual relationship was unsatisfactory, but she said she preferred it to a relationship with a man. She was sophisticated about psychodynamics, and depicted the etiology of her interest in women as being due to both idealization of her brother, and having had an incestuous relationship with him. She had married her husband because he reminded her of her brother, but she also was reminded that it felt dangerous to have sex with a man.

"I'm scared of men, basically. Women are safer."

"Might you be scared of sex?'

"Sure, although I like it, sometimes. I mean, sometimes I go back to my husband. He never remarried. Those times, we have sex."

"Are you scared then?"

"A little. I don't know. Probably not that much. I know it is a temporary thing." "Is it a temporary enjoyable thing?"

"It has its moments, but I think it is mainly a way of keeping a connection to him. No, more than that, to being married, or at least being bisexual, which looks like, you know, then I'm not really a lesbian."

"You don't sound happy with who you are."

"I am. You are wrong about that. I need the confusion. It helps me. I'm not really straight either, and I don't want to be. Now you've got it?"

"Probably not. I am used to thinking either-or, I guess."

"Yes, me too, actually, but I don't want to think that way, so, at least I do not act that way. Of course, it would be easier to be straight, in some ways, but being a lesbian is safer."

"So this is about protecting yourself?"

"I think you are getting closer. I don't protect myself well, though, because I fight with people, I put them off, I'm difficult, and sex is just one part of it."

This woman illustrates different sexual preferences. Her need to do this appears to be defensive, with her sexuality uncertain and disappointing. Her difficulties are not because she is a lesbian, or bisexual, or whatever she prefers. Her sexual identities are a result of other issues, such as vulnerability, trauma, and a need for both confusion and safety.

A distinction can be made between defensive sexuality in which sexual preferences are expressed primarily because they protect the person against noxious affects, and the same sexual preferences that are expressed because they demonstrate the most satisfying sexual identity. It is not sexuality itself, or the particular sexuality, that is problematic, but what the sexuality means to the person, and to others. This view takes into account a certain degree of normal defensiveness that may result in a protective sexuality as distinguished from defensive sexuality in which the distortions are marked.

Because the norm for sexual identity remains heterosexual in most societies, there is a tendency to focus on developmental problems that might result in any identity other than heterosexual. Factors such as traumatic experiences, distant parents, and biological abnormalities, are cited as possible causes. Are gay men likely to have distant fathers? Some, but that situation is not unique to gay men. Nonetheless, the pathways to pathology have characterized explanations of sexual orientations other than heterosexuality. In contrast is the view that there are normal pathways to numerous sexual identities. This has been emphasized particularly by analysts who contend that healthy homosexuality is equivalent to healthy heterosexuality as a developmental possibility. However, as far as we can discern, they do not explain sufficiently the origin of preferences. For example, Isay (1989) points out the error of designating all homosexuality as pathology. He depicts a normal pathway of same-sex erotic fantasies using the Oedipal situation in a traditional manner, but the father is the primary sexual object. Identification with the mother contributes to "feminine" traits. The erotic attraction to the father is attributed to constitutional factors. The explanation then relies on biological essentialism, which is not supported by research evidence (DeCecco & Shivley, 1984). At most, one might suggest a constitutional predisposition, but that is not a predetermination. Also, this approach ignores the polymorphous aspect of sexuality, as well as the strong interaction of both genders with their mothers, which makes them the more likely initial erotic objects. Insufficient attention is paid to interactions between instinct, personal attractors, and social constructions, which is basically the way we conceptualize the normal pathways to sexual orientations.

Another attempt at such description (Minton & McDonald, 1984) begins with the differentiation of self from others. This is considered a period of sensitization to sexual experiences which creates a foundation for an orientation and a sense of individuality, but reasons for such sensitization are not suggested. Then there is a stage where social norms are internalized and influence identity formation. This is considered a period of signification which heightens awareness of sexual roles and their consequences. The latter may contribute to a discrepancy between sexual feelings and a sexual identity that isn't the norm, and subsequent identity confusion. This stage is followed by a critical evaluation of social expectations and the establishment of a sexual identity. This identity can first be accepted, then acted upon, and subsequently integrated with other parts of the self. This is a model that is applicable to any sexual orientation, although it was first proposed for homosexuality. The major limitation is the lack of detailed explanation of the origins of the erotic feelings in the sexual identity, the "why these attract, why these do not."

The lack of specification is understandable, but any theory remains incomplete without further attempting to understand the etiological possibilities. Reductionism, particularly to biological essentialism, does not work, so we have to face the complexity of the issue. There are multiple variables reflecting the interaction of constitution and experience. We designate them as personal attractors that give meaning and specificity to desire, the essence of instinctual sexuality. At the same time, others (Gagnon & Simon, 1973) have emphasized the social construction of a particular desire from the many possible bodily gratifications. This contributes to the understanding of preferences for both sexual objects and activities. The choice of specifics can be seen as dependent on the meaning an individual gives to the possibilities available.

Thus, sexual activities that are unusual exist because of personal attractors. Sadism and masochism, for example, may be motivated by the mixture of sexual desire and the desire for power or for submission, that can be traced to a need for control, or a feeling of safety when controlled. Of course, the concept of sexual attractors is also integral to "usual" sexuality. Sexual intercourse can be experienced as the fantasy of the original unity of mother and child, or as a merger with any idealized other.

Sadomasochism is an enactment of a fantasy involving pain, either given or received, attached to sexuality to the degree that it enhances sexual pleasure. The same idea can be applied to transvestism. As one patient described the situation:

"I can look like a woman, feel what it would be like to be a woman. But I can also be a man. I can have my penis and eat it too. What could be more exciting?"

Or frightening, because sexual experiences often include disturbing components, such as aggression, as well as fantasies or behaviors that might be considered odd, e.g., fetishes or particular bodily positions. The unusual or extreme nature of these behaviors tends to result in the people who are involved experiencing anxiety about them. This occurs because they do not fit the normal social construction of sexual contact and may be categorized as perversions, or "weird, strange, etc." However, such anxiety is usually misplaced because perversity, in some form, permeates sexuality. Sexual intercourse is, in certain ways, frequently an aggressive activity in which demands are made by each partner on the other, as well as being a process of submission for each partner. Thus, there is usually some sadomasochistic flavor, but it is not acknowledged. Then, the particulars of sexual interaction usually have fetish aspects, translated into, "this is my favorite way to be in this situation." The need for "special conditions" is usually accepted without discussion, provided the range of what is needed seems "okay enough." The idea that the "setting" is in essence a fetish is not considered.

The result is that there are many ways to have sex that are acceptable to the parties involved. They do not seem so unusual as to disturb the people doing them, nor are they harmful to anyone else, but they are idiosyncratic and could be considered perversions based on their deviation from a social norm for sexual behavior. Then there are more extreme or unusual behaviors that "push the envelope," but are essentially harmless and acceptable to the people practicing them. These are technically perversions, but once the people involved can deal with the guilt of being unusual, these could be enjoyable and should not be considered pathological. Finally, there are sexual behaviors that disturb the self or others in a variety of ways. These need modification.

The explanations for the attractions of unusual sexual behavior, particularly in its more intense forms, such as the association of pain with sexual pleasure, lie in experiences that established a connection. These experiences may or may not be traumatic, but they always have sufficient impact to create the appeal. For example, spanking, which would seem to be a form of punishment, can be that and more, as sexual excitement may also occur. The latter may be a result of sensory contact as well as fantasies regarding the personal meaning of the spanking. These experiences, intended to be one thing, become another. They have an incidental effect, which can occur for any of the people involved. Some action becomes sexualized despite its customary non-sexual function. At first, it may be just associated with sexual excitement, but then it usually becomes sexually exciting. The reasons for the act being sexualized are often not apparent and not remembered, although people may recall when the association began. Although these actions, or fantasies, are not experienced as sexual by many people, they are very sexualized for some. The sexual part is reinforced over time and becomes a strong personal attraction or a need. This indicates that almost anything can get sexualized, which, by now, should come as no surprise. The issue becomes, when is that a problem and when, in contrast, can it be integrated into acceptable sexual behavior.

Sexual Problems and Sexual Offenses

A sexual problem occurs when a person's sexuality has a toxic effect on the self or others. Thus happenings such as premature ejaculation, erectile dysfunction, inability to have an orgasm, lack of desire, sexual obsession, insensitivity to the needs of sexual partners, confusion about sexual identity, and shame and guilt in regard to sex, are all sexual problems. These are only some of the possibilities. The defining characteristic is self-limitation of one's sexuality. The etiology of these problems usually lies within the developmental process, can be discovered through the analytic process, and can be changed.

Sexual offenses are sexual behaviors that are illegal and whose destructive characteristics are clearly apparent. These activities are sex crimes, such as sexual assault and child molestation that in addition to being sexual problems, involve a superego meltdown. People carrying out these behaviors are considered sexual offenders who often are arrested, or at risk for arrest. Although their behavior involves sexuality, and may include sexual pleasure, it seems more hostile to others, and to the self, than sexual. The sexual part appears primarily as the mode of expressing aggression.

Now the behavior fits the concept of pathology. Pendergast (2004) notes that etiological possibilities can usually be found in contributing factors such as sexual trauma, parental abuse and neglect, and a generally disturbed childhood. The result is a distorted use of sexuality as a vehicle to serve needs that are not primarily sexual. In searching the developmental history, the likely finding is a perceived connection between the aim of the offense and the use of sexual behavior to achieve that aim. In that regard, Pendergast (2004) suggests a connection between the need to control and sexual behavior, as well as the presence of sexual trauma, although he admits that there is not a definitive answer to the reason for the choice of sexual behavior over some other mode of realizing the person's aim. Finding the answer remains a challenge.

Another concern is making the distinction between sexual offenses and sexual behavior that contains elements of being problematic that could result in offensive behavior. Healthy sexuality operates within a social context containing limits. This is exemplified in the concept of Freud's id, ego, and superego interacting and operating as an integrated system. Unfortunately, a distortion has taken place where the emphasis has been put on developing a sexual norm that contains bias, as well as pathologizing behavior that deviates from this norm. Instead, it is of greater interest to try to understand how each person's sexuality develops, the influencing factors, and the aims of the sexuality. Of course there is value in being able to predict and prevent sociopathic uses of sexuality, but there is not a clear formula available to do this, nor is there likely to be, given the complexity of the issue. The developmental potential is for sexual diversity in form and goal, but sexuality is embedded within biological, relational, and cultural factors that shape personal meanings and behaviors. Thus the degree of diversity of sexuality, akin to aggression, will be restricted. At issue is whether the adaptation is a healthy or pathological one. Interest in the entire range of desire is considered normal, as differentiated from a socially constructed arbitrary norm that has heterosexuality and masculine superiority as its core. Although less widespread than in the past, it remains the primary norm. It would be a significant improvement if what was normal about sexuality, namely its diversity, became normative. Unfortunately, the obstacles to that are formidable, beginning with the fear of being different and the current disdain of such differences. Perhaps a more plausible possibility is that what is normative be viewed as a statistical concept rather than a health concept. At least, that way, what the majority thinks or does would not automatically determine what is or is not pathological.

The support for heterosexuality includes normality, health, social expectations, and in many instances, moral beliefs. The formidable support, however, does not make other sexual life styles unhealthy, just different. The uphill quality of the battle for responsible sexual freedom is striking, but so was the struggle for women's rights, and in both cases, improvement has taken place. Psychoanalysis, as a premier comprehensive theoretical possibility for explaining sexuality, ought to be in the forefront of the battle. That means no hiding behind some of what Freud said, or almost said, or burying sexuality in relationality, attachment, or mutuality. Self-object relations and a sexual self that is inserted amidst the other selves to the point of being incidental is not sufficient either, nor is a reformulation of Lacan's reinterpreted imagined phallus.

Sex is given notice in all the theories and concepts mentioned, but it is getting lost. Its significance as a vital part of a person's identity is being dissipated. A return to the raw stuff, real sex, and the role of sexuality in the individual's development, is needed. Sexual desire will continue to be socially constructed in order to be expressed and accepted, but the forms and shapes of passion require renewed recognition. After all, the creators of pornography get their ideas from the same pool of fantasies available to everybody. Sexual fantasies can be limit stretchers, frightening in their apparent perversity, intensity, attraction, and freedom. It is an understatement to say it is worth giving them some thought. It is also worth remembering that the thought is not equivalent to the action, and that the actions to be considered are not sexual offenses, but involve the accurate acknowledgement of enjoyable, responsible sexuality.

Some recognition has happened. Significant changes include the reinterpretation of the psychosexual stages to better understand women's sexuality and de-emphasize phallocentrism, the de-emphasis on a type of natural sexuality that made object relations incidental to sexual discharge, and the social recognition of gay, lesbian, and bisexual relationships. However, these will be insufficient if reconstruction stops there, and if the thrust of these considerations gets marginalized in the mainstream theory, which happens too often. The comments by Decker (2004) alluding to building sandcastles for lesbians as a positive development in the spirit of Stephen Mitchell seem to be a poignant attempt at transforming relational theory into something that is sexually enhancing. Unfortunately, it is not, and it is no more gay or lesbian friendly than its theoretical predecessors, which, for a while at least, were somewhat sexually obsessed.

Consider Harris's comments; "I would still want to inquire why psychoanalysis has been so recalcitrant and so impenetrable to internal criticism in regard to homosexuality"(1995, p.xiii).

Take this inquiry a step further, substitute "the range of sexualities" for "homosexuality," and there is the basic question, still unanswered. We are looking for psychoanalytic theories that do not avoid the question, and that try to provide answers even when they are relatively obscure or assumed, but this is acknowledged . In addition, the theories will try to provide more of an answer than has been forthcoming. So far, the main answers have been forms of biological essentialism or social construction that are open to significant criticism and turn out to be inadequate.

QUEER THEORY

Earlier we mentioned queer theory as an approach that is more welcoming to sexual diversity than other psychoanalytic conceptualizations. Queer theory originated in other disciplines and has been borrowed by psychoanalysis. Grossman (1992) provides an excellent summary of the theory which describes its derivation from feminist theory, gay and lesbian studies, and philosophy. The theory does away with the idea that having a fixed sexual identity is a developmental necessity. It also involves a debate between essentialists and social constructionists, but now about the origin of a flexible sexuality, with constructionists explaining sexual identity in a cultural context.

Although the vision of queer theory is appealing, we have already noted that its scope appears limited to only some sexual identities. Turner (2000) seems to make a similar point in suggesting that the flexibility of constructionism creates more options than envisioned by queer theory. Leaning in the direction of constructionism, Grossman sees a compatibility with psychoanalysis in regard to the influence of the unconscious on erotic preferences. The unconscious serves as the container for the unknown or unrecognized determinants of object choice. This explains the frequently reported patients' feelings of "always felt this way, must have been there from the start," which could be perceived as akin to essentialism. However, the contents of the unconscious are primarily repressed material, experiences that once were conscious. As a result, the meaning of the experiences is not available, but that does not indicate the meaning was predetermined.

The reasons for the unconscious determinants having such a powerful effect, given that they are in competition with other, contrary determinants, both conscious and unconscious, is not explicated in detail. Some attribution is given to the power of social forces in the culture exerting unconscious influences on sexual preferences. The possible roles of interactions with caretakers and the environment are downplayed. There is an attempt to avoid making social construction appear to be a causal explanation. It is depicted more as understanding in a cultural context, but, at the very least, that borders on the etiological.

Jagase expands queer theory by noting "its definitional indeterminacy, its elasticity" (1995, p.1). She also suggests that the relation between chromosomal sex, gender, and desire are probably the effects, rather than the origin of sexual preferences.

Thus, three linchpins emerge to connect the origins of sexual preference with its determinants, and all have limitations. The three are biological essentialism, unconscious cultural influences, and personal attractors. The first is not well supported by research evidence and seems the weakest explanation, backed mainly by selective feelings of predetermination and social convenience. The possibilities of biological influences and predispositions of character, however, remain in consideration. The second is presented more as a description than a cause, although it contains etiological implications. It also does not offer enough specifics, but does highlight the significant influence of sociocultural factors. The third accepts the possibility of aspects of both the first and second having an influence, but puts the emphasis on personal conscious and unconscious experiences. However, it is currently limited by the need to discover specifics and the reasons for their impact relative to other influences.

Conclusions

Despite reformulations, psychoanalysis tends to view sexual preference as determined by same-sex parent identifications that include opposite-sex object choice. This is based on a family model consisting of a female mother and a male father with each having an erotic preference for the other. In turn, the children in the family will imitate the gender preference of the same sex-parent. Although the original polymorphous character of sexuality supports cross-identifications as well as same-sex erotic preferences, these are believed to be essentially sublimated as part of the Oedipal resolution.

Such a belief is designed primarily to support a traditional family structure that emphasizes a norm of heterosexuality and sexual intercourse aimed at reproduction. It leaves little room for the existing variety of instinctual and learned erotic interests. Normative sexuality has been equated with health. Other sexual preferences and possibilities have been considered pathological.

However, for some time now, such a view of the normative has been challenged by a number of sources, such as feminism, queer theory, aspects of a number of psychoanalytic psychologies, as relational and self, and by sexual minorities resisting designation as aberrant. The result has been some significant progress in opening the discussion, but with unfortunate contextual reservations. For example, same-sex relationships have been released officially from pathological designation, but marginalization remains. Women's sexuality has a new viability where its expression and formation are better understood, yet a phallocentric slant is prevalent in the culture. Gender equality often has dramatic impact, but has to coexist with reluctant acceptance. Sexual diversity struggles for acceptance, makes some gains, then has to struggle again with backlash because the progression creates anxiety about what the changes will bring to society.

In psychoanalysis the need to establish the healthy reality of sexual diversity has overwhelmed the need for understanding the developmental pathways to the variety of viable sexualities. Theory has lagged the presence of diversity and the need for the acceptance of its existence. This is understandable, but it is time for theory to be reformulated. For example, in establishing the importance of relationships, the instinctual aspects of sexuality and its motivational importance were neglected. Alternatives prevailed over integration. Biological essentialism gained popularity as an explanation for the etiology of marginalized groups wanting authenticity, as opposed to considering the probability of different developmental approaches.

A more likely explanation for sexual diversity is that biology presents a variable potential, and people-factors take it from there, often in ways that are unexpected and confusing, but quite insistent. A key factor in sexual development is the experience of personal attractions. These are based on conscious and unconscious influences that are singularly powerful. The reasons for these powerful appeals are often mysterious and will require individual analytic investigation to create the possibilities of discovery and understanding Such exploration needs to take place in the context of recognizing potential sexual fluidity, the possibility of healthy and defensive sexuality, and the personal and social difficulties of acting in accord with sexual desires.

Chapter 5

INTEGRATION

In a landmark book in 1983, Greenberg and Mitchell set in motion an alternative view of motivation, the relational model. As part of their elaboration, they described this approach as incompatible with a drive model, so that they essentially dismissed the idea that motivation can be derived from both relational and instinctual sources. The relational focus gained acceptance, and then momentum. The alternative became a contemporary theoretical preference based on the belief that such a theory was better than its predecessor.

Superiority has ultimately been asserted by proponents of major alternative approaches. Their signature belief in different primary motivations creates exclusivity, and, in turn, undue restrictions on the role of sexuality. In drive theory the emphasis has been on drive discharge, which diminishes the relational aspect of sexuality. In contrast, relational theory makes the drive secondary to the mode of sexual experience.

Neither of these approaches by themselves are satisfactory explanations of sexuality. We disagree with the value of such a reductionistic conception as a valid explanation for motivation. In 1990, Pine presented the case for a multi-model perspective, which involves a hierarchy of motivation in each individual. Unfortunately, this view never gained ascendance, and the importance of sexuality has been diminished, thus depriving psychoanalysis of an opportunity to arrive at a comprehensive view of motivation in general and sexuality, in particularly.

The resurrection of sexuality depends on the acceptance of the multiplicity of motivation, a position we have endorsed in earlier work (Herron, 1999). Our clinical experience is in accord with Pine's suggestion, also clinically based, that one size does not fit all. Motivations are individualized, layered in terms of importance, and subject to shifts.

Our impression is that resistance to the expansiveness of motivation in psychoanalysis is based on a tradition of reductionism, the possible efficiency of that approach in terms of understanding and application, and the personal preferences of the model makers. Dual and single motivational models have been the most popular, whereas multiple models have garnered a limited following. Nonetheless, we believe that a multiple model is most congruent with clinical experience. Our first step in offering a revised psychoanalytic theory is to consider sexuality as one motivation within an indefinite number of motivations so as to allow better understanding of the different patients now likely to come to our practice. Since these patients come from diverse cultural backgrounds, analysts will be better equipped to address the issues of motivation and sexuality in the context of these patients' unique cultural experience.

Furthermore, we consider sexuality to be both instinctually and experientially derived, and to vary in quality and quantity on an individualized basis. Its prominence appears on a hierarchical ladder shifting across people as well as within each person, so it is context-dependent. The components of sexual expression have constitutional roots appearing in sexual energy and excitement level, and interpersonal origins seen in sexual fantasy and interaction with others.

The result is that we consider sexuality to be everything that Freud said it was, and more. We consider it to be a drive, but not exclusively aimed at discharge because the creation and maintenance of sexual excitement is satisfying as well. This means that sexual activity is part of the energy system involved in bodily processes; essentially the physiology of the body doing something the person considers to be sexual. Sexuality is a psychobiosocial phenomenon, with psychoanalysis focused primarily on the psychological factors involved in the biosocial surround of sexual experience.

Our next concern is the proclivity for sexual partners and sexual activities. We consider sexuality originating as polymorphous desire. The internalization process shapes the choice of sexual orientation. Although the nature of sexuality means that there is a choice of both partners and activities, adaptation to both the availability of objects and the acceptability of activities and objects, is a major determinant. The ego and the superego control the activities of the wishes of the id, but not desire itself, which is influenced by conscious and unconscious personal attractors. These are formed by both predisposition and experience in the process of developing identifications that lead to identity formation. Conflict appears in the adaptive process when desire clashes with reality or social and moral forces.

The prevalent norm is heterosexual, but patterns of normal development also exist for other orientations, as homosexuality and bisexuality. The differences lie in the personal attractors and types of identifications that have the most appeal to each individual. Sexual conflicts occur when the behavior involved becomes problematic for the self. This may be due to personal anguish, or causing harm to others. In all instances, sexual behavior needs to be understood on an individualized basis, and the analytic process is an ideal instrument to do this.

A viable psychoanalytic theory of sexuality conceptualizes psychic development as a path to flexibility in sexual fantasy and behavior. The analytic clinical goal is gaining the greatest *acceptable* sexual freedom for each individual. "Acceptable" has a contextual meaning, namely, "that depends." The variables involved are myriad, but can be distilled into general categories of personal, social, and moral norms of approval.

Personal refers to what the self evaluates as, "this is me" behavior that fits into a desired self-image. The personal view is influenced by what the culture considers acceptable, which in turn incorporates moral values. The three categories are interconnected, with the self serving as a filter for acceptability. Within this arena of self-approval there are sexual interests and activities that fit easily into the existing personality structure, and there are other possibilities that the person considers risky or dangerous, although still in accord with their value system. In addition, there are possibilities that have appeal, but fall outside of personal guidelines for approval. These may be put into action, but provoke guilt that can limit satisfaction. Finally, there are sexual behaviors that are so unacceptable to the person that they will not occur. These are either outside of the person's area of interest or knowledge, or despite an interest, their unacceptability predominates.

Working analytically with a person involves the analyst being aware of sexual acceptability, and then understanding the patient's sexuality in that context. A key factor in doing that successfully is the analyst's own feelings about sexuality. The issue of countertransference will be revisited in detail later in the chapter. Before that, we want to consider the possible reasons for patients engaging in particular forms of sexuality.

Sexual Motives

There are a host of reasons for seeking sexual satisfaction. We will describe some of them that are consistently prominent. In general, there is a sensory appeal. The sensation that occurs feels good. This may occur based on the physical contact, or it may include symbolism. In the former, the pleasure is due to the sensation, much as it would if the person were eating or drinking. In the latter, the act also has a meaning. For example, in intercourse, penetration may signify a connection indicating safety or closeness. Each act can have meaning, so each act can provide bodily gratification and the fulfillment of a wish. The symbolic part may be conscious and unconscious.

Pine (1990) notes that sexuality includes sensations that are inevitably attached to cognition, as well as a history of personal experience contained in mental representation. Diverse aims are met, so in addition to sensual pleasure, sexuality may operate as a defense, enhance self-esteem, facilitate relationships, and provide an outlet for various aspects of aggression. It is over determined and personalized on the basis of personal experience, which rests upon an instinctual foundation. Before the elaboration of this view by Pine, similar attempts were made by Loewald (1971) and Sandler (1981), but the coexistence of the instinctual and the relational as motivational forces never developed significant traction.

The over determination of sexuality creates much of the mystery regarding the origins of sexual specifics. While the biological base of sexual desire appears to be close to a universal, the particulars of desire are variable. They appear to be primarily a function of personal interactions in which a link develops between the sexual drive and certain mental representations, feelings, and actions. The mode of favored sexual expression, including actions and orientations, results in both usual and unusual approaches that are dependent on the individual's personal history.

For example, a person could prefer masturbation to sexual intercourse because greater control of the sexual response is possible, and because there is greater freedom to engage in narcissistic pleasure. The only person who has to be pleased is the self. This behavior could also be considered defensive, if, for example, it occurs because of fear of intimate relations with others. However, it is possible to prefer sex with one's self for reasons other than anxiety about relating. Sex does not have to be part of intimate relations, nor do such relations have to be part of a satisfactory sexual experience.

However, although most people tend to begin their sexual activity with some form of self-stimulation, they then move to physical contact with others as a preference, so there must be perceived advantages. Contact, connection, attachment, intimacy, mutuality, intersubjectivity, and the possibility of reproduction are examples. However, people can be inherently sexual, and inherently social, but the two do not have to be mixed. As we noted with intimacy, sexuality can be a form of socialization, and frequently is, but it does not have to be. When there is interaction with another, the motivations involved are what determine the degrees of relating and sex that are experienced.

The analytic work involves understanding the reasons for the sexuality. Although there is practical interest in determining whether particular sexualities are healthy or pathological, the main focus of analysis is facilitating sufficient awareness of the motivations and meanings of sexual behavior. Understanding makes it possible to determine what is problematic. For example, guilt may limit sexual pleasure, but the problem may be the guilt rather than the sexual activity. Understanding also makes change possible if change is desired or required as it also facilitates an effective therapeutic alliance and relationship.

Each pattern of desire has its own developmental pathways, but the central components are similar. They begin with an instinctual polymorphous sexuality that has the potential for considerable diversity. Then sexuality develops toward a genital primacy whose form of expression is shaped by social constructions involving both intrapsychic and interpersonal adaptation. Internalization moves through introjections and identifications into the formation of an identity. Sexuality includes the establishment of a preferred orientation and preferred behaviors that become customary, but are potentially fluid.

Options other than normative heterosexuality are more prone to cause conflicts for a person because of the social pressures designed to keep the norm in place. However, that does not alter the analytic aim. Interest in same-sex partners, or bisexuality, will reveal the same processes at work as in heterosexuality, but the attractors will be different. Psychoanalysis has not been uncomfortable with conflict, but with the unfamiliar, such as alternative normal sexual orientations. The concept of polymorphous perversity has been more acceptable than the idea of polymorphous sexuality being a customary point of origin. Intrapsychic and interpersonal influences are easily given greater weight than social constructions and multicultural creations, but it is becoming more apparent that sexuality is a function of all these factors.

In the original formulations of sexual development, an assumption was made that people *should become heterosexual,* because that fit the evolutionary concepts of that time, as well as the cultural views that supported the traditional family structure. This framework wasn't questioned. Instead, it was reinforced. Although the "natural" way for the child was sexual diversity, parents were customarily both models and enforcers of supposedly "natural" styles of sexuality that were actually restrictive social constructions. Superego anxiety has been a major weapon in differentiating sexuality to put the child on the "correct" path. What had been natural for the child in the pre-oedipal years, became not so natural in the resolution of the oedipal situation. Sexual training replaced toilet training as the next phase of socialization.

However, it has become clear that society can both survive and thrive with the presence of sexual diversity as a personal option that could be quite healthy with regard to the general functioning. This applies to sexual behaviors as well as sexual orientations. Responsible sexual freedom is comprehensible in a psychoanalytic developmental framework or metapsychology. There is no one formula for healthy sexuality, but psychoanalysis offers a way, on a person-by-person basis, to explore, and then explain, each individual's sexuality. The key question now is, as analysts, are we up to the task? An indication of the problems involved appears in the next section where we explore the issue of countertransference to the patients' sexuality.

COUNTERTRANSFERENCE

The Dream

The male patient addresses the female analyst. "I'm embarrassed about telling you this. I don't really want to tell you."

"If you are not ready?"

"I doubt I'll ever be ready, but I need to talk about it."

"All right."

"You asked me what I really like to do sexually, and I lied. I mean, I didn't tell you the whole story."

The analyst waits. She wonders if she wants to hear it. There are aspects of this man that she does not like. He seems overly impressed with himself, and always trying to impress her regarding his wealth and power. She suspects he doesn't like her, or women, all of whom he seems to view as objects to provide him with pleasure.

"All right, I left out the masochism." He pauses, seems more uncomfortable. Then he adds, "What I really like is masochism."

In her mind she adds, "in women."

He asks, "Are you surprised?"

Her immediate reaction is to think, no, I expected this, and I am not going to like the details. Nonetheless, she suggests he continue.

"I thought you would be surprised." He pauses, then continues. "Oh, but I guess you can see through the façade."

She thinks, this is what I expected, and I do not like men who do this. She wonders, should I really be trying to work with this guy?

He goes on. "I know I came on strong, but, well you probably know this, but I don't feel so strong."

She feels she is about to state the obvious, but that she should encourage him to talk. "You act strong because you feel weak."

"Sort of, but not exactly. It is more that I force myself to appear assertive, dominant, but I wanted to be controlled. I am really a masochist, but I only show it in sex."

Before she can stop herself the words slip out. "You are?"

He laughs now. "I think I had you fooled. It was probably all the hassling I did with you about your fee, and then always wanting to change the time of my appointments. I wanted to piss you off."

"That is what it felt like."

"Sure, but I did it hoping you would punish me. The thought of you spanking me I find very erotic."

She felt he was saying this to upset her, to see if she would be unable to deal with him. Before, he had seemed embarrassed. Now he seemed relaxed and in control. She felt uncomfortable, with an increasing sense of uncertainty as to what to do next.

In an effort to reflect some composure and not appear destroyed by what she was experiencing as an attack on the boundaries of the relationship, she said, "I'm not sure where you are going with this."

"I have sexual fantasies about you. About us, really, in which I am your slave."

She couldn't believe it. She moved away from the possibility of hearing the fantasies to asking him about historical material, namely the possible origins of his interest in being punished by spanking and finding it sexually exciting. He obliged, and the rest of the session was taken up with that material.

She felt as if she had dodged a bullet. Had he somehow sensed her disdain for his style and was trying to make her feel guilty? There was no way, she thought, that this man would allow a woman to do anything other than wait on him. She just did not believe him.

Before she saw him again her opinion was augmented by a dream. In it, the patient was lying across her lap. His buttocks were bare. She was methodically striking his buttocks with a black strap. The words she remembered saying in the dream were, "You deserve this, you know." She awoke, sexually excited, and then felt ashamed. She did not like the picture of herself being violent with anyone, although she did think, that guy deserves some retribution for being the way he is. She did not explore her sexual reaction. It was very unexpected. She did not want to think about it.

She did realize that the patient reminded her of her first husband. She had divorced him once she realized the extent of his dependency. It was draining her. His needs were always paramount. Now she was married to a man who had great respect for her and focused on pleasing her. The attitude carried over to sex. She was dominant, although she had never even imagined getting sexually excited by punishing him.

When she saw the patient again he returned to the issue of his fantasy of her dominating him sexually. He said that he was wondering If he should not have told her, and that if he was out of line, he apologized.

This made her feel worse. "Out of line," she thought. I encouraged him to be open with me, and now my reaction is making him feel as if he cannot say what he is thinking.

However, she remained dubious about his expressed interest in being a masochist in any situation. She asked him, "Did you feel you offended me?"

"I realized I may have."

"How did I give you that impression?"

"Well," he said, "maybe it is your technique, but you didn't really address what I brought up."

"You mean," she asked, "your feelings about me?"

"My sexual feelings about you," he noted.

She felt furious with him. It was as if he knew about her dream, and he would add to her guilt about it. He was making her into someone she did not want to be.

"All right," she said, "let's talk about those feelings." She could feel the tension in her body as she said the words. She had a sexual desire she must have hidden from herself, and then this patient that she does not like, forced her to look at it.

"We don't have to," he said, "if it upsets you."

She snapped at his words. "Are you patronizing me?"

She saw fear in his face. He said, "Look, I'm sorry. I didn't want to make you angry this way. The other stuff, it was part of my fantasy, but I want you to like me. The thought of you spanking me as part of the therapy, it was outrageous. That made it more exciting."

She felt as if he was waiting for her to tell him if he could continue. She thought that his apology could be a way to get her to agree to let him go on assaulting her. She could not seem to let go of the feeling that he knew about her dream, and worse, that he had the power to sexually excite her by describing his sexual fantasies.

Although the silence was brief, she experienced it as very painful. She broke it by saying, "Please go on. It is all right."

She knew it was not, but hoped it could be. She also knew her own unexpected sexual arousal had gotten in the way. Her feelings were split in a number of directions.

It would be easier if he decided to stop seeing her. If he continued, she was likely to think further about the sexual role she had played in the dream. That was a previously unrecognized part of her that she felt she would now like to disown. His continuance would mean she would have to be more open to him, and to herself.

If she could not do that, if he was going to be too much for her, she would have to find a way to tell him that would not do more damage. He was talking, but not about his fantasy. She sensed she had frightened him, and that his attraction to a masochistic position could exist and cause him to stay with her and sexualize the analytic process, but not tell her. She knew she would be compromising the work if she let that happen. Although afraid, she decided it was time to stop having secrets from herself.

She said, "I pushed you away. If you don't mind, let's go back to your fantasy about me spanking you."

He appeared surprised, but agreeable. "Sure," he said, "but is it all right with you?"

"It is important." She thought, you tell me your fantasies and I will have mine, and we will see where that takes us.

The Rejection

The woman had never married, rarely dated, and had never engaged in sexual intercourse. It was as though she had been asleep for 50 years, busy caring for her mother who had recently died. She mourned, but also came alive, suddenly it seemed all she could do was think about sex. These words never left her, "I want to get laid."

Her discomfort with this dramatic shift brought her into analytic therapy. Her male analyst seemed very patient and understanding. He helped her see the probable connections between her sexual repression and her life with her mother, to whom she has certainly been devoted. She found the analyst's gentle approach very appealing. She was attracted to him, and she considered that there was at least a possibility that he might be attracted to her. The pursuit of "getting laid" never left her.

She told the analyst about it, using the words because by now they were so familiar, although foreign to the way she usually spoke.

The analyst said, "Well. It is understandable that you would have strong sexual feelings."

"Yes. Yes. I suppose it is, but the way I keep thinking about it bothers me."

"It is understandable that you might feel obsessed right now,"

"Obsessed?"

"Yes. Isn't that the way you are feeling?"

She supposed it was, but when he used that word he seemed colder to her, more clinical. Then she dismissed the idea that he was being distant. He was right. She was obsessing.

As the weeks passed she continued to have the same thought, but a dimension had been added. She now wanted to get laid by the analyst, but did not mention that part. She faithfully informed him of the repeated thoughts of wanting sexual intercourse. He did not appear to react negatively to her revelations, nor did he use the word, "obsessed," again. Instead, he encouraged her to talk more about her desire. The idea that he had ever attempted to be distant she now dismissed. However, she was reluctant to tell him that he had become the object of her desire. She created a fantasy person to describe and talked about having sex with him. However, given that she had little experience to draw upon, her descriptions were limited as to specific sexual activities.

He asked her, "Are you afraid to talk about this?"

"Yes," she said, "I am."

"The phrase you used was, 'get laid.' Is that what you are doing with this man, and you are afraid to describe it to me?"

"I don't know how to describe it, especially to you."

"Especially to me?"

"Yes," she said, and then the rest of it tumbled out. "You are the person I want to get laid by." She closed her eyes after she spoke.

"That would not be possible," he said. "You can open your eyes. Nothing terrible is going to happen because you told me."

But, she thought, something terrible just did happen. Her eyes were opened by his words. She was silent as she struggled with her thoughts. Should she tell him she felt rejected? No, she thought, because of course he was right, it was not possible. They could not have a sexual relationship. She always knew that, but she did like to imagine that they could, anyway. She liked to think that he could have the same feelings about her that she had about him. His words had taken all that away. Correct as he might be, she felt crushed, and he really did not seem to be aware of what he had done to her.

"The truth is too hard," she finally said.

"I know is it very difficult for you to tell me your fantasy. I appreciate your strength in doing that. It is important that you feel free to tell me all your feelings."

But, she thought, now I don't, and you are misunderstanding my reaction. It was the truth you told me that was painful, not what I told you. Why did you have to say, "That would not be possible?"

In this case we only know the story from the patient's perspective. After that session, which she described as, "mercifully coming to an end," she called the analyst. She left a message that she needed some time to recover from her revelations, so she would not be coming in for a while. He returned her call, leaving a message that he understood that she had been upset, but that he felt it would be best if she returned to discuss her feelings. If she was not ready to do that now, she should call him when she was. She never called him. She felt he was relieved to have her leave.

It appears that the analyst was uncomfortable with the woman's sexual fantasies. The first sign of this was his use of the word, "obsessed," which made her uncomfortable. Although he may have been correct, there appears to be no clinical need for using the term. Given that he does not continue to use it after she questions him, it is probable that he realized the usage was not helpful. It is unclear whether he also recognized that his words could be a function of his own need to try to limit the discussion. That need becomes more probable when he subsequently emphasizes to the woman the impossibility of sexual contact between them. His reaction is tempered by his willingness to discuss her fantasy, but he anticipated a need to state a boundary that he did not know the patient was really intent on crossing. Would she have crossed it given the opportunity? It would seem so, but he did not have to give her that opportunity, and that did not require that he tell her at this point that there would be no opportunity. He may have been anticipating that she would subsequently ask him about his feelings for her, which also seems quite possible. If that happened, then he could have responded in a more effective way. It appears that either he had sexual feelings for her, but wanted to make sure she did not know this, or he did not, and wanted to make sure she knew that. Regardless, he seems out of touch with the impact his reactions to her sexual feelings would have on her. As a result, the analytic work with him was stopped because the patient felt too injured. In her view, the analyst's comment was not a necessary orientation to reality, but a painful rejection of her sexuality just as she was beginning to experience it.

The Proposal

The male analyst found a young female patient particularly appealing. He felt his enthusiasm for he was very helpful in their work. Over a period of a few years she had made progress in both her career and the avoidance of destructive relationships that had plagued her in the past. It was his impression that she was quite attracted to him, although she had never reported directly any sexual desire for him. There were at least two dream sequences in which she featured the analyst as a potential marital partner. In both instances her associations suggested these dreams were about her relationships with her parents. She had a number of involvements with men, and it became clear that she was choosing people who would not work out for her. She had sexual relations with these men, bit this was not the focal point of their relationships, and she spent little time in analysis discussing her sexuality. The analyst's impression was that for her, sex was something that came along with serious relationships, but was not of much interest to her.

Nonetheless, he found her sexually attractive and attributed her reticence to the limitations of her partners as well as a strict upbringing by both parents. He considered her compassionate, caring, and intelligent. He began having thoughts about how good a partner she would be for him. He knew they were both pleased about the results of the analytic work. He felt it was growing close to termination, although he did wonder about aspects of her, particularly sexuality, that had been explored minimally. He considered that it was possible he wanted the analysis to end so that he would no longer be her analyst.

About six months before he began having sexual fantasies about the patient, the analyst had ended his second marriage. The sexual relationship had never been vibrant, and ultimately deteriorated. He considered his wife to be a depressed, chronically unhappy woman who viewed sexual intercourse as a male desire that she would condescend to satisfy infrequently. In contrast, the patient seemed to be a flower who had just begun to bloom. At that point she was career-oriented and without a serious relationship. He felt he sensed an opening, although in the past he had always believed such possibilities should never be acted upon. Somehow, this became different, particularly if the analysis were ended.

The patient then provided a further opening. She was given a promotion to a position that involved additional work, which would make regular analytic sessions difficult. She asked him if he thought she was ready to terminate anyway. If not, she added, she would try to work something out, but it was going to be inconvenient for both of them. Although he knew there was some unfinished business, he told himself that no analysis covers everything. He also sensed it would make her happy to essentially be declared healthy, and he would be glad to have her in a category other then patient.

He was in a peer supervision group, and he discussed the case there. He was somewhat guarded as to his intentions, but made it clear that he wanted to have a relationship with the woman after she was no longer his patient. His colleagues were against the termination, unless he felt he could not handle the case at this point, and were even more against his attempting to have a social relationship with the woman at any point. He reacted to their comments with partial dissociation. He thanked them for their input, told them she appeared to have decided to terminate for a while until she saw how her work schedule was, and thought that they did not understand how he and the woman actually felt about each other.

Although he was aware of the probability of a strong positive transference on her part, he went into denial regarding its impact and duration. He convinced himself that if he waited an appropriate, but undefined, interval after the termination, they could have an authentic romantic relationship. He and the patient agreed to meet for another month to wrap up things. He felt this was an opportunity to clarify their feelings about each other.

The next session he mentioned that he was aware that they had developed a bond between them. She agreed, saying she cared for him very much, really appreciated all he had done for her, and believed that if she needed her in the future, he would be there for him.

He believed she was afraid to say more, that she was holding back unconsciously, so he tried to make it easier for her. He told her that he cared for her very much to the point that he could imagine that they were having a relationship outside of this one.

She seemed surprised, and upset by his statement. She said, "That is not how I care for you."

Now he was also upset and surprised. So convinced was he that she must have sexual feelings towards him that he told her she indeed had them. He suggested that she just was not letting herself talk about them.

It was as though an unknown person took possession of her as far as he was concerned. Her face became stern and she stated flatly, "No, I don't have a sexual interest in you, not at all in the way you seem to be implying. I resent what you have just done. You have ruined this. I am going to leave now."

She went. He called her, left messages of apology, but, that was it. She probably did have some sexual feelings about him during the time they were together, and may have still had them at the end, but they were transferential. She recognized, much more than he did, that they were not about the analyst as a real person. His desire got in the way of what he always seemed to know in the past.

The Connection

The patient's interest in other women was what the analyst found so intriguing. The analyst had considerable training in feminist theory and a strong commitment to advancing women's rights. The patient's potential as an activist had an allure. As a result, the analyst frequently found herself discussing her own opinions about issues they both deemed worthy of great involvement. Afterwards, she would review the session and be unhappy with the way she inserted herself.

As they moved further into the analytic process the patient described an affair she was having with a woman. The analyst, who could describe herself as bisexual in interest, but heterosexual in action, found herself caught up in the fantasy of being sexually involved with the patient. However, she was clear with herself that this was a fantasy she was not interested in putting into action.

The patient was seductive. She formed a rapid and intense attachment to the analyst and often verbalized her interest and affection. She made the erotic part of it very clear, and she also managed to elicit a great deal of small personal information from the analyst. She used this data as informational opportunities to present the analyst with little gifts timed to coincide with significant times in the analyst's life. The analyst accepted these and even reciprocated to some degree, seeing what was happening as small indulgences that had limited transferential implications. After all, the patient had been to a series of analysts, male and female, before this. They sounded as though they had all behaved in a traditional manner that the patient viewed as excessively distant. The patient reported not finding them helpful, so there appeared to be a clinical reason for providing a different experience. The specifics of that difference were what became a very difficult issue.

The analyst was feeling uncomfortable. She wanted the different experience to be therapeutic and analytic. She would periodically wonder if her own interest in the patient and the patient's blatant interest in her were not what was governing the interaction.

Then the patient started to move away from the woman she was involved with in favor of another woman who showed interest in her. The analyst asked, "What appeals to you about this woman?"

Her reply was, "Are you jealous?"

The analyst was surprised. Although she was not jealous, she felt her fantasy had been exposed, and that her own behavior must have led to the discovery.

She asked the patient, "Why did you ask me that?"

The patient laughed. "Fooling around, but, well, you know, powerful women usually find me attractive."

The analyst smiled, and said, "Let's go back to my question."

The analyst recognized that she was not ready at that time to talk about her relationship with the patient, and that the patient had tried to divert her from discussing a significant change in the patient's life. The diversion appeared to be a resistance, but the analyst felt she had contributed to the development of an atmosphere in which the patient had too much control over the flow of the material. As a result it was as though there was no such entity as resistance, and possibly there was no transference, or countertransference either, as far as the patient was concerned.

Not so good, she thought, and as the sessions continued she became more centered, staying with the patient's feelings about significant issues, keeping her own views out of discussions, and generally reducing the indulgences. The patient noticed, and complained.

The analyst knew she had been seduced by the patient into staying away from the therapeutic relationship and accepting a more social interaction. Part of her liked this arrangement, at times may have preferred it, because it permitted a mild indulgence of her sexual desire for the woman. However, what she wanted more was to be effective at the work. At first she thought she was developing a connection that would do just that, but she had been mistaken. Instead the woman had flirted with her and tried to stay away from significant issues causing her anxiety, particularly the way she related to others.

The analyst said to her, "When we met I took note of your previous therapy experiences. It seemed as if you never had the right connection. I made a point of trying to have that happen. In the process we both got somewhat lost in how we were getting connected. We have to keep looking at our connection, reevaluate it, and that is what is happening. We need to make sure it is a therapeutic connection, one that will really help you. We are connected, but I believe now it is more in a way that will work better for you."

"For you, you mean."

"I miss how we were, but if we stayed that way, we would be standing still therapeutically. That is not what you came here to do. And yes, it is not what works for me, either."

In this case the analyst recognizes that they both have been playing too much unproductively, and working too little. She knows she has to change that. This patient is not going to go easily into a work mode, and the analyst was on target in needing to provide a different therapeutic experience. As a result, there will be more experimentation to improve their connection, but the analyst is in touch with her sexual interests here, and knows enough to keep them out of the way of the work that can be accomplished.

Synthesis

Throughout this book we have attempted to make the case for what could be considered a natural sexual diversity. Our basic assertion is that if analysts are sufficiently open to their clinical data, they will see that when it comes to sex, people are all over the place in their desires. Applied to theory, this means the development of metapsychologies that accept the health of sexual diversity and successfully explain its many pathways. We see psychoanalysis as the best opportunity to do this, and we have elaborated theoretical reformulations for this purpose. Our suggestions, as well as their possibilities for implementation in practice, are reviewed in the first part of this chapter.

Then, because successful practice is markedly dependent on the analysts' own reactions to both their sexualities and those of their patients, we highlighted four examples of the role of countertransference. In addition, there is a general countertransference that is a reaction to the many aspects of sexuality that are primarily social constructions. Particular notice has to be taken of a tendency to polarize sexuality on a good-bad dimension. A considerable amount of sexual behavior is viewed in such a context, with good sexuality usually represented by a restrictive framework. What is essentially a matter of social custom has been turned into a matter of health. Disapproval of certain sexualities is expressed by having them designated as pathological. In addition to making too many people suffer needlessly, this approach has obscured the potential normality of sexual diversity. The idea that sexuality is a threat to social order and moral values has been overdone. We end with the hope that attitudes will be congruent with information in shifting toward greater understanding and appreciation of sexual diversity.

REFERENCES

Beebe, B. & Lachmann, F. (2002). *Infant research and adult treatment: Co-constructing Interactions.* Hillsdale, NJ: Analytic Press.

Benjamin, J. (1998) *Shadows of the other: Intersubjectivity and gender in Psychoanalysis.* New York: Rutledge.

Blanck, G. & Blanck, R. (1994). *Ego psychology. Theory and practice* (2nd ed). New York: Columbia University Press.

Butler, J. (1993). The lesbian phallus and the morphological imaginary. In J. Butler (Ed.), *Bodies that matter: On the discursive limits of "sex"* (pp.57-91). New York: Routledge

Collins, P.H. (2000). *Black feminist thought: Knowledge, consciousness, and the politics of empowerment* (2nd ed). New York: Routledge.

Damasio, A. R. (1999). *The feeling of what happens: Body and emotion in the making of consciousness.* New York: Harcourt.

Daniluk, J. (1998). *Women's sexuality across the life span: Challenging myths, creating meanings.* New York: Guilford Press.

DeCecco, J. P. & Parker, D. A. (1995). The biology of homosexuality: Sexual orientation or sexual preference. In J.P.Dececco & D,A. Parker (Eds.), *Sex, cells, and same-sex desire. The biology of sexual preference (pp. 1-27).* Binghamton, NY: Harrington Park Press.

DeCecco, J. P. & Shavely, M.G. (Eds.)(1984). *Bisexual and homosexual identities. Critical theoretical issues.* New York: Haworth Press.

Decker, B. (2004). Building lesbian sandcastles on the shore of relational psychoanalysis. In J.M. Glassgold & S. Tazenza (Eds.) *Lesbian, feminism, and psychoanalysis: The second wave* (pp. 79-93). Binghamton, NY: Harrington Park Press. Dimen, M. (2003). *Sexuality, intimacy, power.* Hillsdale: Analytic Press.

Elise, D. (1999). Primary femininity, bisexuality, and the female ego ideal: A re-examination of female developmental theory. *Psychoanalytic Quarterly,* 66, 489-517.

Enns, C.Z. (2004). *Feminist theories and feminist psychotherapies. Origins, theories and diversity* (2nd ed). New York: Haworth Press.

Fast, I. (1984). *Gender identity. A differentiation model.* Hillsdale: Analytic Press.

Fonagy, P., Gergely, G., Jurist, E. & Target, M. (2002). *Affect regulation and neutralization: Developmental, clinical, and theoretical perspectives.* New York: Other Press.

Fonagy, P. & Target, M. (2003). *Psychonalytic theories. Perspectives from developmental psychology.* New York: Brunner-Routledge.

Francoeur, R.T. & Noonan, R.J. (Eds.). (2004). *International encyclopedia of sexuality.* New York: Continuum.

Freud, S. (1914). On narcissism. An introduction. *Standard edition,* (Vol.14, pp. 73-102). London: Hogarth Press.

Freud, S. (1905). Three essays on the theory of sexuality. *Standard Edition, Vol.7, pp. 125-145.* London: Hogarth Press.

Gagnon, J.H. & Simon. W. (1973). *Sexual conduct: The social sources of human sexuality.* London: Hutchison.

Grasz, E. (1999). *Jacques Lacan: A feminist lntroduction.* New York: Routledge.

Green, A. (1996). Has sexuality anything to do with psychoanalysis? *International Journal of Psycho-Analysis,* 76, 871-883.

Green, V. (2000). Emotional development-biological and clinical approaches-toward an integration (pp.1-20). In V.Green (Ed.), *Emotional development in psychoanalysis, attachment theory, and neuroscience.* New York: Brunner-Routledge.

Greenberg, J. (1991). *Oedipus and beyond: A clinical theory.* Cambridge, MA: Harvard University Press.

Greenberg, J. & Mitchell, S. (1983). *Object relations in psychoanalytic theory.* Cambridge, MA: Harvard University Press.

Grossman, G. (2002). Queering psychoanalysis. (pp. 287-299). In J.A.Winer & J.W.Anderson (Eds.), *Rethinking psychoanalysis and the homosexualitiies.* Hillsdale, NJ: Analytic Press.

Harris, A. (1995). Foreword (pp. xi-xiv). In T. Domenici & R.C. Lesser (Eds.), *Disorienting sexuality: Psychoanalytic reappraisals of sexual identities.* New York: Routledge.

Harding, C. (Ed.) (2001). *Sexuality: Psychoanalytic perspectives.* New York: Brunner-Routledge.

Herron, W.G. (1999). *Narcissism and the relational world.* Lanham, MD: University Press of America.

Isay, R.A. (1989). *Being homosexual: Gay men and their development.* Northvale, NJ: Aronson.

Jacobson, E.(1984). *The self and the object world.* New York: International Universities Press.

Jagose, A. (1995). *Queer theory. An introduction.* New York: New York University Press.

Kaplan, L.J. (1994). *Female perversions.* Northvale, NJ: Aronson.

Kascoff, B. (2004). The queering of relational psychoanalysis: Who's stopping whom? *Journal of Lesbian Studies,* 8, 159-176.

Kernberg, O. (1976). *Object relations theory and clinical psychoanalysis.* New York: Aronson.

LaDoux, J.E. (1996). *Thee emotional brain: The mysterious underpinnings of emotional life.* New York: Simon & Schuster.

Levine, R. (2004). Afterthoughts: Comments and reactions to the N.I.P 15th annual conference: Shame and sexuality. *Psychoanalytic Perspectives,* 2, 101-105.

Lichtenberg, J. (1989). *Psychoanalysis and motivation.* Hillsdale, NJ: Analytic Press.

Linqiardi, V., & Drescher, J. (2003) (Eds.) *The mental health professions and homosexuality. International perspectives.* New York: Haworth Medical Press.

Loewald, H.W. (1971). On motivation and instinct theory. In *Papers on Psychooanalysis (pp.102-137).* New Haven: Yale University Press.

Lyons-Ruth, K. (1991). Rapprochement or approchement. Mahler's theory reconsidered from the vantage point of recent research on early attachment relationships. *Psychoanalytic Psychology,* 8, 1-23.

Mahler, M., Pine. F. & Bergman, A (1975). *The psychological birth of the infant.* New York: Basic Books.

Meissner, W.W. (1993). The self-as-agent in psychoanalysis. *Psychoanalysis and Contemporary Thought,* 16, 459-495.

Meissner, W.W. (1999). The self- as-subject in psychoanalysis. I. *Psychoanalysis and Contemporary Thought,* 22, 155-201.

Meissner, W.W. (2000). The self as structural. *Psychoanalysis and Contemporary Thought,* 23, 373-416.

Mendoza, S. (2001). Genital and phallic homosexuality. (pp. 153-169). In C.Harding (Ed.), *Sexuality. Psychoanalytic perspectives.* New York: Brunner-Routledge.

Metzler, D. (1979). *Sexual states of mind.* Strath Tay: Clunie Press.

Miller, J.B. (1976). *Toward a new psychology of women.* Boston: Beacon Press.

Minton, H.L. & McDonald, G.I. (1984). Homosexual identity formation as a developmental process (pp. 91-109). In J.P. DeCecco & M.G. Shavley (Eds.), *Bisexual and homosexual identities. Critical theoretical issues.* New York: Haworth Press.

Mitchell, S.A. (1988). *Relational concepts in psychoanalysis.* Cambridge, MA: Harvard University Press.

Money, J. (1999). *Principles of developmental sexology.* New York: Continuum.

O'Neal, J.M., Good, G.E. & Holmes, S. (1995). Fifteen years of theory and research on men's gender role conflict (pp. 146-206). In R.F.Levant & W. S. Pollack (Eds.), *The new psychology of men.* New York: Basic Books.

Parker, D.A. & DeCecco, J. P. (Eds.)(1995). *Sex, cells, and same-sex desire: The biology of sexual preference.* Binghamton, NY: Harrington Park Press.

Phillips, A. (1998). *Winnicott.* Cambridge, MA: Harvard University Press.

Pine, F. (1990). *Drive, ego, object, and self. A synthesis for clinical work.* New York: Basic Books.

Prendergast, W.E. (2004). *Treating sexual offenders.* (2nd ed). New York: Haworth Press.

Raughton, R. (2003). The International Psychoanalytical Association and homosexuality. *Journal of Gay and Lesbian Psychotherapy,* 7, 189-196.

Rizzuto, A., Meissner, W.W. & Buie, D.H. (2004). *The dynamics of human aggression. Theoretical foundations, clinical applications.* New York: Brunner-Routledge.

Russo, R. (1997). *Straight man.* New York: Random House.

Ruth, D. (2004). Engorging the lesbian clitoris: Opposing the phallic cultural unconscious. *Journal of Lesbian Studies,* 8, 177-189.

Sander, L. (1985). Toward a logic of organization in psycho-biological development (pp.20-36). In K.Klein & L.Siener (Eds.), *Biologic response styles: Clinical implications.* Washington, DC: American Psychiatric Press.

Sandler, J. (1981). Unconscious wishes and human relationships. *Contemporary Psychoanalysis,* 17, 180-196.

Scour, R.C. (2001). *The body bears the burden: Trauma, dissociation, and disease.* New York: Haworth Medical Press.

Sigura, D.A. (2001). Challenging the Chicano text: Toward a more inclusive contemporary causa. *Signs. Journal of Women in Culture and Society,* 26, 541-550.

Stein, R. (1998). Review of the psychoanalytic theory of sexuality. *International Journal of Psychoanalysis*, 79, 988-995.

Stoller, R. (1985). *Presentations of gender.* New Haven: Yale University Press.

Stolorow, R.D. (1997). Dynamic, dyadic, intersubjective systems: An evolving paradigm for psychoanalysis. *Psychoanalytic Psychology,* 14, 337-346.

Stern, D. (1985). *The interpersonal world of the infant.* New York: Basic Books.

Turner, W. (2000). *A genealogy of queer theory.* Philadelphia: Temple University Press,

Weeks, J.(1995). History, desires, and identities (pp. 33-50). In R.G.Parker & J.H.Gaguan (Eds.),*Conceiving sexuality.* New York: Routledge.

Winnicott, D.W. (1965). *The maturational process and the facilitating environment. Studies in the theory of emotional development.* Madison, CT: International Universities Press.

INDEX

C

D

Q

R

S

T

U

V

W